D0045464

RISING ABOVE

INSPIRING WOMEN IN SPORTS

Also by Gregory Zuckerman

with Elijah and Gabriel Zuckerman

RISING ABOVE: How 11 Athletes Overcame

Challenges in Their Youth to Become Stars

RISING ABOVE

ABOVE

Inspiring Women in Sports

GREGORY ZUCKERMAN

with Gabriel and Elijah Zuckerman

PHILOMEL BOOKS

PHILOMEL BOOKS

an imprint of Penguin Random House LLC
375 Hudson Street
New York, NY 10014

Copyright © 2018 by Gregory Zuckerman,
Gabriel Zuckerman, and Elijah Zuckerman.
Penguin supports copyright. Copyright fuels creativity, encourages diverse
voices, promotes free speech, and creates a vibrant culture. Thank you for
buying an authorized edition of this book and for complying with copyright
laws by not reproducing, scanning, or distributing any part of it in any form
without permission. You are supporting writers and allowing Penguin to
continue to publish books for every reader.
Philomel Books is a registered trademark of Penguin Random House LLC.
Library of Congress Cataloging-in-Publication Data is available upon request.
Printed in the United States of America.
ISBN 9780399547478
1 3 5 7 9 10 8 6 4 2
Edited by Brian Geffen.
Text set in 12.5-point Apollo MT Std.

To the superstars in our lives—

Savtah Ricki, Savtah Tova,

Aunt Aviva, Aunt Shoshana,

and, of course,

Mom

CONTENTS

SIMONE BILES

At the age of two, Simone Biles was taken from her mother.

Shanon Biles, who suffered from drug and alcohol addictions, never properly cared for Simone and her three other kids. Simone's father had abandoned the family and wasn't around. With Shanon absent much of the time, too often there was no one looking after the children.

Shanon was arrested multiple times during Simone's childhood. Twice, Shanon was caught stealing cases of baby formula at a local Target store; another time she was arrested for shoplifting children's clothing. Since her four children were left alone so often, regularly playing in the streets in their Columbus, Ohio, neighborhood with no supervision, neighbors began calling social services, urging the city to step in to help Simone and her siblings.

Some of Simone's earliest memories were of hunger pangs. Even when she visited relatives, Simone had a hard time finding enough to eat. Once, she visited her uncle and poured tap water into a bowl of cereal because there was no milk in the home.

Even at a young age, Simone became frustrated by her living conditions.

For most girls, a visit from a neighborhood cat brings joy. But when a local cat sauntered by Simone's yard, she felt resentment—the cat seemed content and well fed even as Simone and her siblings struggled for food. Years later, Simone would still feel antipathy toward cats, though she knew her feelings weren't justified.

"This cat was always being fed—and at the time, we were hungry a lot, so I was always kind of mad at this cat," Simone recalls in her book, *Courage to Soar.*

One day, a social worker came and sat with the four kids on the front steps of their house.

"We're placing you kids in foster care so Shanon can try to get better," the social worker said.

As they sat in the back of the car, driving away from their home, Simone and her siblings were too scared to speak, a searing memory that remained with Simone the rest of her life.

Little Simone was frightened as she prepared for the unknown, moving in with a group of strangers. Simone soon realized she had nothing to worry about. Living with her foster family, Simone and her siblings enjoyed three full meals a day for the first time and got to play with a backyard swing. Simone remembers soaring high and doing backflips after jumping off the swing midair, amazing onlookers who couldn't believe someone so young was attempting such daring tricks. Her foster parents, whom Simone called Miss Doris and Mr. Leo, wouldn't let little Simone jump on their trampoline, however, because they were worried she might get injured. Simone watched with envy as the family's older, biological children somersaulted with glee off the trampoline.

Simone's foster parents "were doing their best to

keep us safe but I just knew I could do the moves the older kids did," Simone recalls. "I was always running and jumping, cartwheeling, and somersaulting."

On Christmas Eve 2002, when Simone was five, she got a real surprise. Her grandfather Ron Biles brought her and her siblings to live with him and his second wife, Nellie, in Spring, Texas, about thirty miles from Houston.

It wasn't supposed to be a permanent thing. The family hoped Simone's mother could kick her addictions and learn to care for her kids. But an attempted reunion ended after Shanon failed new drug tests. The following year, Simone's grandparents legally adopted her, along with her younger sister, Adria, while their two siblings moved in with Ron's sister.

At first, Nellie had been reluctant to adopt the girls, unsure how they'd integrate with her existing family. She also worried she wouldn't be a good mother. Nellie prayed that she could love Simone and her sister as much as she loved her own sons.

It turned out there was no need for concern. "I don't know the exact date [it happened]," Nellie says, "but my heart just made room" for Simone and her siblings.

Simone felt loved. She began calling her grandparents Mom and Dad. Finally, she was well fed and cared for.

"I was happy," she says. "I knew because the knots I usually felt in my tummy were gone."

There even was a trampoline in the backyard of her new home. Simone bounced, twirled, flipped, and somersaulted for hours, her beaded braids flying. She tried different moves, some quite daring, to see if she could land on her feet. She usually succeeded.

Simone's situation was unusual, but she embraced it. "I thought every kid was adopted . . . to me it's just normal," she says. "I want to know why my mother did what she did. But those aren't questions for me because that was her lifestyle [before I was] even born."

One day, when Simone was five, her day care center decided to take the kids on a field trip to a farm. It rained that day, however, so they changed their plans and headed for a gym called Bannon's Gymnastix in nearby Houston.

From the moment she entered the gym, Simone was enthralled. She was tiny for her age but the equipment seemed perfect for her size—there were low beams and a low bar along with floor vaults and mats. Simone saw someone jump backward, use her hands, and then land while standing upright—something gymnasts called a back handspring—so she tried her own backflip. Simone pulled it off, over and over again, landing on her feet each time and even adding a little twist at the end.

A woman who worked at the gym raced over, amazed at what she was seeing from such a young girl. She gave Simone a few simple instructions, telling her to point her toes and keep her knees together, and invited Simone to come back to the gym for some formal classes. Before long, gymnastics consumed Simone's life. Practice, gymnastics classes, more practice, and even more classes. She couldn't get enough.

Fearless, surprisingly strong, and full of energy, Simone had discovered the perfect sport for her personality and body type. Even at such a young age, a local coach, Aimee Boorman, believed that with hard work Simone had a chance to develop into a special talent.

"Her physical stature and her energy are what caught my eye," Coach Boorman says. "The biggest obstacle with coaching her was her desire, or lack of desire, for repetition. Most high-level gymnasts are comfortable with doing very high numbers of repetition, but not so much in Simone's case. Luckily, she didn't require them."

As Simone worked to perfect her routines, she noticed her body changing and her muscles expanding. Some kids teased Simone about her bulky, well-built physique. Even in the world of gymnastics, small and powerful wasn't seen as an ideal body type at the time.

As she got bigger and stronger, Simone turned self-conscious. "I definitely wasn't one of the cool kids," she writes in *Courage to Soar*. Sometimes when she was around young people her age, Simone wore baggy clothing, such as an athletic jacket on top of her outfit, to mask her muscular physique. "I always hid it," Simone later told *New York* magazine.

Spending more time in the gym with others focused

on the sport helped Simone build confidence. It took a while but the more she practiced and succeeded at gymnastics, the more she learned to ignore how others viewed her.

"Once I started going to the gym more, I realized that . . . it wasn't weird. I have these muscles because I do the sport that I do," she says.

The critiquing of her body and her abilities never quite stopped, though.

In 2013, Simone turned sixteen and began competing in the senior elite category of amateur gymnastics. She dealt with early challenges, including difficulties with the horizontal bars. Legendary coach Martha Karolyi once watched Simone practice and told Coach Aimee Boorman that "this kid has no bars . . . She can tumble great, but that's it."

Coach Boorman encouraged Simone to ignore the criticism and keep working to improve her technique. "Her family and I always told her that she could stop doing gymnastics whenever she wanted," Coach Boorman says, "but if she was going to put her energy in it, she should try to be the best that she could be."

Simone took the lessons to heart. Soon, she began dominating competitions and gaining broad acclaim, especially after winning gold at meets in Italy and Germany. Sometimes, she didn't even need to be at her best during practice to win subsequent competitions.

In July 2013, Simone traveled to Hoffman Estates, Illinois, to compete in the Secret US Classic, a meet that's a tune-up for the USA Gymnastics National Championships. At the Secret competition Simone would face real pressure for the first time. Nearly eleven thousand fans packed into the Sears Centre Arena to watch Simone compete against 2012 Olympic gold medalists Kyla Ross and McKayla Maroney as well as other top gymnasts.

Early on, Simone fell on the uneven bars and then bobbled and almost tumbled off the balance beam, shocking fans in the stands. Simone still had the floor exercise ahead, usually her strength, so she tried to shake off the early, embarrassing mistakes.

Wearing a multicolored outfit, Simone flashed a

confident smile as she began the floor exercise. She nailed her first few jumps—she was precise in her movements and seemed in control and in sync with the music. Fans and judges could see her upbeat personality, the goal of every competitor in the exercise, and Simone seemed on her way to an impressive performance.

"You got it, Simone!" a fan yelled to encourage her.

Ninety seconds into the routine, however, something startling happened. Simone lost her balance after a jump, landing clumsily. Just twenty seconds later, after attempting a full-twisting double-back somersault, Simone landed so awkwardly that she almost fell on her face. Simone had to put both hands out to protect her face from smashing into the mat.

It was *that* bad.

"Oooh," the crowd shouted, feeling bad for her.

Simone couldn't hide the crushed, despondent look on her face as she left the floor. Unable to stop thinking about her mistakes, Simone felt uncomfortable and awkward as she prepared for her next event, the vault, which would conclude the competition. Simone was so clearly off her game that Coach Boorman pulled her from the competition before she even could attempt a single vault.

"She just about tried to kill herself on her vault warm-up," Coach Boorman told a reporter. "She could have done something that could've ended her career right then and there if I let her compete . . . her mind wasn't where it needed to be."

Simone finished in thirteenth place out of fifteen competitors, the worst meet of Simone's senior career.

"I think I was just trying to live up to everyone's expectations that I kind of got lost in competing," Simone later explained. "I was just so stressed. I didn't know how to deal with a lot of it."

On her way out, Simone overheard another coach critiquing her performance.

"She's too fat," the male coach said. "How does she expect to compete like that? Maybe if she didn't look like she'd swallowed a deer, she wouldn't have fallen."

Humiliated, Simone rushed behind the curtains and cried.

"It was really hard, because growing up, I never

felt overweight or fat," Simone later told *People* magazine. "It shocked me."

Once again, Coach Boorman told Simone to ignore the criticisms. Her weight was the same as when she won earlier competitions. A lack of preparation and conditioning had led to her poor performance, Coach Boorman insisted, not her size.

"You can't train like this and expect the results to show," national team coordinator Karolyi added, shaking her head with disapproval. "I believe in you . . . Turn the page."

Later, when Simone met other gymnasts like gold medalists Aly Raisman and Gabby Douglas she learned she wasn't the only athlete dealing with body shaming.

"You name it and she got trampled," says Gabby Douglas's mother, Natalie Hawkins, in reference to stinging critiques her daughter faced on social media about her hair, her skin, her body shape, and more. "Gabrielle's had her heart broken."

Because female gymnasts usually are young women competing in formfitting outfits, even as their bodies are still developing, they often feel insecure and super-conscious of the opinions of coaches, parents, fans, and others.

"It's hard growing up in a sport where you compete with very little clothing on your body and everyone is staring at [your body] no matter how good you are," Simone says. "People will always say you don't look good *enough*."

Yet over time, Simone learned to ignore the criticisms and snide remarks.

"In a way it actually shaped me for the better," she says, referring to the comments about her weight. "It just taught me to rise above and to love my body no matter what."

Later, when she was an established gymnast, Simone tweeted: "You all can judge my body all you want, but at the end of the day it's MY body. I love it & I'm comfortable in my skin."

To Simone, her poor showing at the Secret was a crushing blow. So many people had predicted she'd have a star performance, and she'd expected so much of herself, but she'd failed. Simone's adoptive mother—by then Simone just saw her as her mother—noticed that Simone started doubting herself and found excuses for her performance. Gymnastics is a tough sport—judges nitpick and search for the tiniest mistakes, Simone's mother knew.

Sensing that she was bottling up her worries, Simone's parents suggested that she meet with a sports psychologist to discuss her worries and frustrations.

"You just turned sixteen and you have the whole world looking at you and they expect a certain level of performance," Coach Boorman said of Simone in an interview with writer Dvora Meyers. "You're not a normal kid, and you don't have normal problems."

At first, Simone resisted seeing the psychologist. "You all think I'm crazy," Simone said, according to her mother.

Eventually, she agreed to go. The psychologist taught Simone various strategies to handle her stress, such as breathing techniques. They were invaluable tools for an athlete because in sports, mental toughness is just as important as, if not more important than, physical toughness.

Her coaches gave her sharp criticisms after the Secret event. Instead of reacting with anger or hurt, however, Simone viewed the coaches' comments as pep talks and helpful critiques. The coaches still believed in her and Simone knew they were right about how she needed to improve her practice habits.

"Simone made up her mind that she was going to be great," Coach Boorman says. "She didn't want to have another performance like that."

With the national and world championships ahead, Karolyi invited Simone and Coach Boorman to the Karolyi Ranch in Texas for one-on-one training sessions. Karolyi told Simone that the difference between being a great gymnast and a world-class competitor was the practice necessary to get to the next level. But Karolyi also told Simone that it's okay to fail. Take a chance, try to win the upcoming competitions, but if it doesn't happen it's not the end of the world, Karolyi said.

Individual attention from Karolyi helped improve

Simone's mental outlook, as did continuing work with the sports psychologist. The pressure building on Simone seemed to lift. She decided to get back to enjoying herself.

"You kind of just knew that if you went out there and made a mistake, that it's okay," Simone says.

Just three months after her embarrassing performance at the Secret Classic, Simone traveled to the Sports Palace in Antwerp, Belgium, the world's second-most visited event hall after New York's Madison Square Garden, to compete in the World Championships against stars around the world, including Kyla Ross, who had won the Secret.

Simone and Ross went back and forth, vying for the gold medal, Simone's strength and athleticism matched by Ross's polish and elegance. Both had scores of about 60 points and Ross led by just 0.016 points ahead of the final floor exercise. It would come down to this one, last event.

Wearing a bright pink outfit, Simone launched into a powerful routine. Her landings weren't perfect. Her toe-point needed work—gymnasts receive a 0.10-point deduction just for failing to point their toes. But fans were wowed by Simone's powerful effort; thousands in the crowd rhythmically clapped along to the music as Simone leaped, twisted, and strutted. Simone left the floor with a huge smile. Ross was smooth and graceful, making hardly any mistakes, but her routine couldn't match Simone's physicality and degree of difficulty.

The results flashed on the stadium's board as the competitors embraced—Simone finished with a score of 60.216 points, edging out Ross at 59.332 points. Simone had won the all-around gold medal, the first African American woman to become all-around champion. And it all took place during her rookie year, no less. Simone had just hoped to make the national team that year, but now she was an international champion.

It was the first of three world all-around titles Simone would win, a turning point in her career. It had been a challenging road from failure to success, but along the way, she learned that trusting her talent, ignoring the critics, enjoying herself, and sharing her concerns with others brought out her very best.

Simone developed a growing and avid fan base, yet

critics searched for a reason to explain away her talent, focusing on her strength and ignoring her obvious grace. Following the world championship victory, Italian gymnast Carlotta Ferlito even suggested that the color of Simone's skin had helped her achieve success and fame.

Ferlito said she and teammate Vanessa Ferrari should "also paint our skin black so that we could win, too." David Ciaralli, spokesman for the Italian Gymnastics Federation, added that black gymnasts are "known to be more powerful," giving them an unfair advantage.

The comments were quickly condemned by fans and others, and Ferlito apologized. But the criticisms pointed to underlying racism in parts of the gymnastics world that Simone still had to deal with, some said.

By 2016, Simone had dominated the world of gymnastics in a way no one ever had. Simone even had perfected a move that no male or female gymnast had ever completed, a double flip in a layout position with a half twist and a blind landing, a move that makes it look as though she's flying. Because only she could pull it off, the move became known as "the Biles."

As the Summer Olympics in Rio de Janeiro, Brazil, approached, Simone, just nineteen years old and four feet, eight inches tall, was the clear favorite. A key reason she was so good: Simone attempted more-difficult routines than almost all of her competitors. In 2006, the sport's governing body rewrote its point system to increase the awards for attempting difficult routines, something Simone specialized in. That change helped Simone.

Simone "attempts trickier elements than anyone, and she pulls them off cleaner than anyone almost every time," the *Wall Street Journal* said. "It's an unbeatable combination."

Early on at the Olympics, Simone anchored a dominant US team victory and destroyed the rest of the field in the individual all-around competition. Simone knew she would have a greater challenge if she was going to win a third gold in the vault. She had won multiple world championships in the balance beam and floor exercise, but never in the vault. In fact, no American had ever won a gold in the event.

Months earlier, Simone was struggling so much with

her intricate and extremely difficult Cheng vault that she resorted to scrapping the move and trying an entirely new vault. In the end, she decided to try to fix the Cheng.

But as Simone walked with Coach Boorman onto the Rio Olympic Arena's floor, the coach sensed Simone was ready for something special.

"She got a little more giggly," the coach told a reporter, "and that's usually her thing."

Simone, the last to perform, aced her Cheng after landing her Amanar vault, both high in difficulty and executed so well that she racked up enough points to blow away her competition. Simone beat silver medalist Maria Paseka of Russia by 0.703 points and bronze medalist Giulia Steingruber by 0.75 points, an enormous difference.

How dominant was the victory? In the two previous Summer Games, the gaps between the gold and silver medalists were 0.108 points and 0.075 points.

Simone came as close to perfection as anyone in the history of women's gymnastics.

"She's definitely the best that I have ever seen,"

said Mary Lou Retton, the legendary gold medalist.

With three gold medals earned, Simone headed into her second-to-last event, the balance beam. Fans started to wonder: Could she do the unthinkable and win gold in all five of her events?

It was not to meant to be. Simone performed well, but she was not the victor this time around. She won bronze, her fourth medal of the competition, but wasn't crushed missing out on gold in the event.

"I'm not disappointed in the medal that I received because anyone would love to have a bronze at an Olympics Games," Simone said.

Simone bounced back to dominate on the beam, unleashing her signature Biles move, finishing the Olympics with four gold medals and a bronze, becoming the fourth American female gymnast to win five medals in a single Olympics.

Simone was selected to carry the US flag during the closing ceremony. So many fellow athletes stopped her along the way to congratulate her or take a photo with her that the closing ceremony was delayed for her arrival.

• • •

Simone's Olympic Games domination amazed the world and resulted in new acclaim. Some called Simone the greatest gymnast ever. Others called her the Michael Jordan of gymnastics.

Even as Simone was cheered around the world, a new challenge emerged. Just after the Olympics, hackers released the medical files of various Olympians, a leak that showed Simone was taking a drug that was on the prohibited list of the World Anti-Doping Agency. The hack was aimed at embarrassing Simone and causing a scandal, but instead of ignoring the issue or denying she had taken the drug, Simone acknowledged taking medication since childhood for ADHD. She had permission for the drug and wasn't ashamed, she added.

"Having ADHD, and taking medicine for it is nothing to be ashamed of nothing that I'm afraid to let people know," Simone tweeted.

Simone wasn't embarrassed about her difference.

"I was born with my body for a reason," she says.

In fact, the same body type that some rival coaches had mocked earlier in her career now was praised.

"Her body is nearly ideal for the sport," the *Wall Street Journal* wrote in 2016.

The compliment underscores an important lesson—ignore critics and doubters and be comfortable in your own skin.

It's no longer "weird" for girls to have muscles, Simone says. "Now people are like, 'Do you lift? Are you a gymnast? You have a good body.' People just appreciate it more, and we're just a little bit more confident as we get older."

Other top gymnasts emphasize a similar message about the importance of embracing one's unique body type.

"Shout-out to all the boys from 5th–9th grade who made fun of me for being 'too strong,'" Raisman posted on Instagram in 2016, after winning a silver medal. "My muscular arms that were considered weird and gross when I was young have made me one of the best gymnasts on the planet. Thanks for forcing me to learn to love myself and my body. Don't ever let anyone tell you how you should or shouldn't look."

Simone hopes young women who feel a lack of

confidence about how they look or are subject to body shaming by peers or others can learn to ignore the negative comments and doubters.

"Don't even listen, love your body!" she says. "You were born with it, God has blessed it. Don't pay attention to negativity."

Today, Simone is taking things day by day and planning the rest of her life. Her biological mother is drug free, and Simone speaks with her from time to time.

"She is a fun, lighthearted young woman who happens to be incredibly talented," says Coach Boorman, adding that Simone hasn't changed very much. "We talk a few times a week and she is still 'just Simone.'"

Simone emphasizes the importance of finding a passion in life, something you can dedicate yourself to.

"I know it sounds clichéd but don't give up on your goals," Simone says.

She shared a tip for how to keep life's goals in focus.

"Write them down, the small ones as well as the big ones. And don't give up on them!"

But it's not only about dedication for Simone—most

important of all is enjoying what you're doing. After a meet once, Karolyi told Simone she was getting distracted and seemed to be enjoying herself too much. "Tone it down," the star coach said. Simone had to explain that when she's happy and smiling, she's in her zone and at her best.

Simone's ability to enjoy the moment doesn't get in her way—it's a key reason she will go down as perhaps the greatest gymnast in history. It's a way of approaching life that can lead to other kinds of success, as well.

"No matter how old you are, it's never too late to start something you love," Simone says. "Do something good with it! Pursue your dreams and passions!"

And most important of all? "Always have fun," Simone says.

ELENA DELLE DONNE

Elena Delle Donne seemed to have hit the jackpot.

Growing up outside Wilmington, Delaware, Elena had remarkable basketball skills even at a young age. At seven years old, Elena played on a team of eleven-year-old boys. She became so good that colleges sent scouts to watch her games while Elena was still in grade school. In the summer after seventh grade, Elena even received a future college scholarship from the University of North Carolina, though she didn't accept the offer.

A star high school basketball player, Elena set a

national record with eighty consecutive free throws and led her team to three straight Delaware State Championships. Elena, who was born to a family of athletes, was so focused on becoming the nation's best female basketball player that she got up at six in the morning to run; later in the day, she'd lift weights and practice shooting. By senior year, Elena had emerged as the top female high school basketball recruit in the country, a six-foot-five force who had the unique offensive ability to excel inside the paint as well as beyond the three-point line.

Geno Auriemma, the legendary University of Connecticut coach, was so impressed that he offered Elena a scholarship as a guard/forward, making Elena the envy of thousands of young female players around the world. Elena was expected to be a key player as the Huskies tried to capture a sixth national title during the 2008–2009 season before crowds in Connecticut that sometimes swelled to ten thousand. It was clear Elena was the next great female basketball star, a life of wealth and fame surely ahead.

But soon after Elena arrived on Connecticut's campus

in the city of Storrs, she was absolutely miserable. She couldn't stop thinking about her family. Yet it wasn't the typical homesickness that many college students experience being away from home for the first time. Elena was unusually close with her family, partly because they had gone through so much together.

Her older sister, Elizabeth, twenty-four years old at the time, had cerebral palsy and autism. Elena had seen Elizabeth endure more than thirty surgeries to try to help her condition. When she was younger, Elena often would go with her sister—whom they called Lizzie— to physical therapy appointments, sitting quietly and playing while Lizzie worked with specialists.

It was clear to anyone who knew them that Elena and Lizzie had a unique bond that only grew over the years. Because Lizzie also was blind and deaf, it was harder for her to communicate. She relied on touch and smell rather than texts and phone calls. As a result, Elena and Lizzie developed their own hand-over-hand sign language. Elena knew exactly when Lizzie was asking for food or drink.

"Feel and smells . . . it's just more of those types of

senses," Elena told a reporter for ESPN. "It is kind of hard to explain it in words, but it's just everything, like our love, our relationship is completely touch and feel. That's how we communicate with each other."

That unique form of communication just wasn't possible long-distance, though. Indeed, Elena said leaving her sister behind to go to college in Connecticut made her so sad it was like "a big piece of my life missing."

"I look up to Lizzie more than anyone else," Elena told the *Hartford Courant*. "She's an inspiration to me."

After just two days of classes, Elena decided she couldn't take the pain of being away from her family.

"I can't do this," she told her parents.

Adding to her misery, Elena began to feel that in devoting so much of her life to basketball, she had missed the opportunity to try other pursuits. She realized she was becoming tired of basketball being the center of her world. All of a sudden, she felt the need to walk away from the sport.

"I was overdriving myself because I was so into becoming the best," Elena said. "It wasn't fun. It was like a job."

Despite all the hard work she had put into her game and her bright future as a member of the Huskies basketball team, Elena made an abrupt decision to leave Connecticut. She was so unhappy that she bolted in the middle of the night, getting a ride home from an old friend, a decision the *New York Times* called "stunning."

According to Elena, "It was tough and I was scared, but I had to do it." She was crying when she got home early the next morning.

Some criticized Elena for squandering her God-given talent and leaving her school and teammates so hastily. There even were rumors that she was on drugs or pregnant and needed to leave campus. Others wondered if Elena would regret her decision to quit the storied basketball program.

Once she was back home, Elena transferred to the University of Delaware but decided to play volleyball. Elena was burned out on basketball and wanted to try a new sport that appeared to be more fun and less stressful. At her new school, Elena sometimes played volleyball matches in front of fewer than two hundred fans, well short of the massive crowds that attended basketball games at the University of Connecticut, but more important to her, she was near Lizzie and her family once again.

Elena wasn't a great volleyball player, but friends said she finally looked happy. Still, her parents had mixed feelings about her new life. They were thrilled to see her smiling once again, of course. But even they weren't sure Elena had made the right the decision to leave Connecticut and the sport she had dominated, jeopardizing her future in the process.

"If Tom Brady was your son, you would really enjoy that he was a darn good Ping-Pong player, but you'd feel like, 'Why's he playing Ping-Pong?'" Elena's father, Ernie Delle Donne, said at the time, referring to the legendary New England quarterback.

In some ways, such second-guessing wasn't new for Elena. She had dealt with criticism from others in the past. For many years, her height bred insecurity. One of Elena's first memories is a trip to the market as a three-year-old. She was so tall that strangers stopped her mother to criticize her for letting an eight-year-old rely on a pacifier.

Later, a doctor said Elena was getting too tall and recommended injections to stunt her growth. Her mother declined the suggestion, but Elena left the office feeling like something was wrong with her. A few years later, Elena was humiliated when she and classmates measured themselves in science class for a project and Elena dwarfed everyone else. Elena looked so different from her classmates that she became uncomfortable.

These moments were embarrassing for Elena, but it was even more devastating when people made insensitive comments or jokes.

How's the weather up there?

You know, you're really *tall.*

Sometimes she felt "like a monster," she later told ESPN.

Because she stood out in such an obvious way, Elena decided she couldn't act out, convinced teachers and others would notice any misbehavior, even if the mischief of smaller classmates escaped notice.

Adding to her angst: At times, Elena felt guilty that she'd been born with so much strength and physical blessings while her sister wasn't able-bodied.

Thanks to encouragement from her parents, Elena eventually became less self-conscious of her height and even proud of her body, but it was a process that took some time.

Rather than dwell on the criticisms of her decision to focus on volleyball, Elena focused on her family and on establishing a new life that worked for her. Delaware's campus was a short ride from Wilmington, so Elena was able to return home during the week and remain part of Lizzie's life. Elena drove Lizzie around the family's property on a golf cart and reestablished their unspoken form of communication. More than ever, Lizzie's strength was an inspiration for Elena.

"She's completely put perspective into my life," Elena told ESPN. "When I see her struggling to get up in the morning, struggling to walk on her own—she can't see, she can't speak. What she's able to overcome throughout a day is incredible. Any challenge I ever face, Lizzie has done way more than that. She's my role model; she's my inspiration; and, when things are tough, I think of Lizzie and realize nothing in my life will ever be that tough."

Other people Elena met also encouraged her. One time, while she visited Lizzie at her school, a woman named Dawn, a basketball fan who had cerebral palsy and used a wheelchair, approached her to say hello.

"Elena, do everything you can with your abilities, just like we do."

The words inspired Elena. Rather than feel guilty about her physical gifts, Elena realized she needed to do the most she could with her abilities, just like her sister and others with physical challenges and differences managed to do.

One evening during the winter of 2009, Elena picked up a basketball, walked into an empty gym with a friend, and began taking shots from all over the court. It felt good to just play without worrying about her future.

I miss that feeling, Elena thought.

With her newfound motivation and a renewed love of the sport, Elena began considering the idea of playing basketball once again. Delaware's women's team had never achieved any kind of prominence, but in some ways that may have been an added attraction for

Elena. She'd be free of the expectations she would have faced in Connecticut, where any season that doesn't end in a championship is seen as a disappointment.

It was time to return to the basketball court—and time to rediscover her love of the game.

Elena picked up where she had left off, dominating opponents almost from the start of the 2009 season, quickly emerging as one of the nation's best players. She averaged 26.7 points per game, third highest in all of Division I women's basketball, including a 54-point performance in a loss against James Madison.

It seemed as though Elena had it all. She was back home with her family, in close touch with Lizzie, and having fun playing basketball again. But before long, Elena would have to deal with another, shocking setback.

The next year, during Elena's sophomore year in college, she suddenly began feeling extremely tired. Often, she slept as many as eighteen hours in a single day. Elena lost thirty pounds and was weaker than ever. It seemed like she had an awful flu that just wouldn't go away. In a game against Penn State, Elena asked her coach for permission to leave the game, the first time she'd ever made such a request.

She couldn't even hold her arms up. Elena began to panic.

"I think I'm dying," she told her parents one day.

For a while, doctors couldn't figure out what was wrong. Eventually, it was determined that Elena had contracted Lyme disease, an infectious disease transmitted by a tick bite that can cause fevers, headaches, fatigue, and skin rashes.

Elena began taking about fifty different supplements to keep her disease under control, though it would flare up from time to time for the rest of her life, draining Elena's energy and occasionally causing her to miss games.

"Keeping my body healthy is like a second job," she says.

The disease wouldn't stop her, though. In 2012, Elena led the nation in scoring, with an average of 27.5 points per game and an impressive 53 percent field goal percentage, while also averaging double-digit rebounds and more than two blocks a game. Elena amazed opposing players and coaches with her ability to go hard all game long and do the little things on the court that many top scorers avoided—fighting for offensive rebounds, rotating on defense, guarding an opponent's top scorer, and more.

During her junior year, Elena once again finished as the league's scoring champion with an average of 28.1 points a game. The next year, Elena led the Blue Hens to a perfect 18–0 record in league play, sweeping through the Colonial Athletic Association tournament. Undefeated, Delaware headed into the National Collegiate Athletic Association (NCAA) women's basketball tournament, playing in front of packed houses, mowing down competitors, and advanced to the Final Four, the school's first-ever appearance. In a matchup against the number two seed Kentucky, Elena scored thirty-three points, but it wasn't enough to secure the win and the Blue Hens fell to the Wildcats. Despite the loss, it had been a historic finish for Elena and her teammates. Even President Barack Obama mentioned Elena when he made his tournament predictions, picking Delaware to advance to the regional finals.

After a game that year, Elena headed to the baseline of the court to greet residents of the Wilmington facility for the disabled, where Lizzie spent much of her time. Elena approached each of the residents with a huge smile and friendly hello before embracing Lizzie, who had been helped out of her wheelchair into Elena's arms.

In that moment, it was clear that Elena had made the right decision.

"To see her just smile and to really enjoy life and enjoy herself, there's nothing better," Gene Delle Donne, Elena's brother, said.

Scouts were so confident of Elena's talent that she was drafted as the number two overall pick by the Chicago Sky in 2013. Elena was excited to join the Sky but also torn by how far she would be from home and Lizzie. She decided to split her time between Chicago and Delaware.

Elena dominated the pros, just as she had in college, finishing her rookie season with an average of 18.1 points per game and earning the Women's National

Basketball Association (WNBA) Rookie of the Year Award. It was the first of many accolades to come.

Elena quickly emerged as one of the top players in the league, winning the WNBA's Most Valuable Player award in 2015, the same year she was named an All-Star for the third time in a row. That year, Elena led the league with 23.4 points a game, ranked third in rebounding with 8.4 a game, and shot a career-high 95 percent from the free throw line.

Elena shared with the *Wall Street Journal* one of the secrets to her free throw success, one that young people can apply to other sports and pursuits.

"I actually just tell myself, 'It's going in,'" she said. "Every single time."

Some began comparing Elena to Dallas Mavericks superstar forward Dirk Nowitzki because she had the ball skills, agility, and shooting touch usually associated with shorter players but she also had the post-up skills of taller players, allowing her to score from almost anywhere on the court.

Elena continued to deal with health issues due to her Lyme disease, however. She began an intensive workout regime, including boxing, running up stairs with weights on her shoulders, push-ups, and pull-ups, improving her endurance in the process. Elena also started avoiding foods that caused inflammation to try to keep her disease under control.

"I think it's always surprising to people that I have a chronic illness and I play a professional sport," Elena told the *New York Times*.

In 2016, she averaged 21.5 points a game, along with seven rebounds, helping the Sky reach the play-offs, though Elena missed the postseason after surgery on her right thumb.

In her free time, Elena began running basketball camps for young people. Inspired by Lizzie's strength, Elena opened the camps to every kind of kid—special-needs children as well as able-bodied players.

Despite her success, Elena continued to feel the tug of home. In 2016, Elena indicated it was time to leave Chicago to play closer to Delaware once again. The Sky complied with her request, trading Elena in 2017 to the Washington Mystics—less than two hours from Delaware—for two players and the second-overall pick in that year's draft, a huge package of talent for just one player and a sign of the respect Elena commanded. Analysts said she was the biggest star ever traded in the league's twenty-one-year history.

"Clearly, this is one of the biggest moves in the history of this organization," Mystics coach Mike Thibault said after the trade. "In only four years, Elena has established herself as one of the premier players in the world, as evidenced by her MVP season two years ago. Her impact on and off the court will be invaluable."

Even though the Mystics had been an underperforming team, Elena was thrilled to be closer to home.

"My entire family is super excited, even aunts and uncles," she said. "I've gotten texts, calls, everyone's thrilled. They'll be at a lot of games. Having Lizzie this close by is so great. Now I'm in such close proximity to her. I'm hoping to get her to a game. She hasn't been to one of my professional games."

Elena also was enthused about her next challenge— helping to turn the Mystics into a winning team. "I'm really excited about this next chapter in my career," she said.

It will be yet another test for Elena. But she's no stranger to adversity. If the past is any indication of what's to come, Elena has a bright future ahead of her. After all, she's faced tough, controversial decisions in the past, proving that with strong will and the right mind-set, she can overcome any obstacle thrown her way.

VENUS AND SERENA WILLIAMS

The tennis courts were damaged, dirty, and sometimes dangerous. Soda cans, beer bottles, and fast-food wrappers had to be swept away before play could begin. Broken glass was everywhere, weeds poked out of the ground, and cracks covered the cement.

Sometimes, gunshots rang out.

Richard Williams told his daughters, Venus and Serena, to ignore the distractions. *Just enjoy yourselves and work on improving your game.*

"Never mind the noise, Meeka," he told Serena,

using her nickname, trying to reassure her. "Just play."

His strategy worked. Most days, Venus and Serena had so much fun volleying with each other that they barely noticed their challenging surroundings. Playing tennis somehow transported Venus and Serena to a calm, happy place.

From these humble beginnings began a lifelong love affair between the Williams sisters and a sport they would dominate like no other two players in history. They would need to overcome a series of unexpected obstacles to achieve greatness, however.

Even before the Williams sisters were born, Richard made a decision about how his future children could build better lives for themselves.

Richard was watching the French Open, one of the four major competitions, or Grand Slam tournaments, in professional tennis, on television in 1978 when he heard something startling. The announcer said the tournament's winner, Virginia Ruzici, had won $40,000.

Richard was amazed—that sum of money was more than he made in an entire year.

Two years later, Richard's wife, Oracene, gave birth to a daughter, Venus. Just over a year later, another daughter, Serena, was born. Almost immediately, Richard vowed to do everything he could to help the girls become tennis stars, just like Ruzici.

Living in Compton, a neighborhood in Los Angeles that was becoming known for gangs and random violence, Richard and Oracene had limited ways of helping their daughters learn the game. The couple didn't have enough money to afford proper tennis clothing for Venus and Serena, and tennis lessons were out of the question.

Serena's earliest memory is of holding a racquet while playing on a court in 1984, when she was just three years old and Venus was four. But the only racquets their parents could get their hands on were much too big for the girls. Richard didn't let the challenges stop his daughters, though. While he couldn't afford formal lessons, he had enough money to order instruction books and videos and taught himself the game so he could share lessons with Venus and Serena.

Most days, the girls played on local courts with their father, as did their three half sisters, who also became passionate about tennis. Other times, Richard drove the girls to public courts a little farther away in a neighborhood where it was rare to see African Americans playing. One day, when Serena was seven and Venus was eight, they were practicing on their own on that court when some local boys ran over and began taunting the sisters about their race.

"Blackie One! Blackie Two!" the boys called out.

Venus and Serena didn't know how to react to the hateful words. Before they knew it, however, their older half sister, Tunde, had chased the boys down and confronted them over their slurs. The boys never bothered the girls again.

"People were used to seeing tennis champions who were white," Venus says in the book *Venus & Serena*. "Who was ever going to believe that two black girls from Compton could become the best in the world? But we didn't stop playing, no matter how wacky our dream seemed to other people."

The five Williams girls had to share a single bedroom with four beds, but the cramped living situation helped them forge a lasting bond. It also encouraged them to empathize with their less fortunate neighbors. Something as simple as having new tennis balls was a luxury the girls learned to appreciate.

"Seeing all parts of life makes you well-rounded and gives perspective," Venus says.

Richard owned a security firm and Oracene was a nurse, but over time their primary focus became helping their daughters become tennis greats. Richard pushed the sisters to excel, but Venus says he didn't force them to play the sport. According to Venus, the sisters were told they could quit if they wanted, but they kept coming back for more, practicing harder each time on the court, several hours each day after school. Soon they came to share their father's dream— they hungered to become champions.

"Daddy believed tennis was our ticket up and out of Compton," says Serena. "But he also knew we had to take to it."

As they grew up, the Williams sisters didn't have

many friends or hobbies, but they continued to improve on the court and enjoyed the sport. Before long, all the practice started to pay off and the sisters began gaining notice for their prowess on the court. They were just one year and three months apart in age, but early on it was Venus—taller, quicker, and more athletic at the time than Serena—who seemed on the fast track to stardom. Venus began winning local tournaments and even drawing attention from national media.

"Venus was the phenom, the prodigy, the rising one," Serena writes in her book, *My Life*. "I understood it on some level . . . but on another level it hurt . . . sometimes it felt like nobody believed in me."

Serena wasn't jealous of her sister. Instead, she vowed to work hard on her game to try to join Venus in the spotlight, at least one day.

For her part, Venus says it sometimes was a burden that so many recognized her talent at such a young age. She felt pressure from both her father and tennis commentators who predicted greatness for her and wondered if she could fulfill everyone's hopes for her career.

"There was a lot of hype and it was hard to balance

my expectations, and the expectations of others," Venus says. "For a young person, that's pressure and it can be hard to navigate."

Venus says she found a solution. She decided to ignore what others predicted for her "and focus on what I wanted to accomplish."

Venus dominated her competition, stunning opponents by winning every match she played as a junior player. She turned professional in 1994 at age fourteen and beat a few top players over the next three years, though she didn't advance far in various tournaments she entered.

In 1997, Venus managed to break into the sport's top 100 ranking. By then, she had gained a following for her style of play—a unique blend of power and athleticism—as well as her distinctive look.

Venus was "like nothing ever seen in tennis before: Beads in her hair, incredible wheels and reach, attitude to spare," *Sports Illustrated* wrote.

That year, Venus competed in the US Open for the

first time and made it to the semifinals, where she played Romanian Irina Spirlea, who was ranked seventh in the world. Amid the excitement, Venus was subjected to an uncomfortable moment on the court. During a changeover in that semifinal match, Spirlea intentionally bumped into Venus, an unheard-of insult that stunned fans and television commentators.

Venus managed to overcome the collision and the distraction it had created, beating Spirlea 7–6, 4–6, 7–6 in a dramatic third-set tie break, even after Spirlea held two match points in the tiebreaker. Later, Spirlea told reporters that she had bumped Venus because Venus seemed arrogant. The move likely also was aimed at intimidating Venus. Venus's father accused Spirlea of racism, an obstacle he felt his daughters were dealing with in a sport that had few black stars.

Rather than get into a war of words, Venus took the high road, telling reporters she wouldn't focus on the collision or Spirlea's criticisms.

"I'm sorry she feels that way," Venus said of Spirlea. "It's not a big thing to me."

The Williams sisters' ability to ignore insults and

distractions would serve them well throughout their careers.

Venus lost in the finals of that tournament, but she became the first woman since Pam Shriver to reach a US Open singles final in her very first try, losing to top-ranked Martina Hingis in straight sets. Months later, Venus beat Joannette Kruger to win her first singles tournament. The following year, Venus avenged her loss to Hingis, then the world's top-ranked female, in a dramatic three-set match at the Sydney International, overcoming cramps in the sweltering heat.

Venus's victory sent a clear message to the tennis world that a new superstar had arrived. She finished 1998 as the world's fifth-ranked female tennis player.

Venus's confidence seemed to grow, even as she played more experienced players. On the inside, however, she still battled insecurities. The next year, she was seeded third in the US Open, but she lost to Hingis in the semifinals.

"On the court, I was just so nervous, I let fear take over," Williams later explained. "And the next thing I know, I'm shaking hands [as] the loser."

Venus vowed to never again let fear get in her way.

"Losses are just awful, they're massive," Venus says. "But the only tragedy of losing is not learning from it."

It took Serena slightly longer than her sister to reach tennis's upper echelon. Unlike Venus, Serena lost several matches as a junior. For a while, she was viewed simply as Venus's kid sister. But Serena made up for lost time and joined Venus as a pro in 1995, at age fourteen.

Just three years later, Serena "announced herself to the tennis world," according to *USA Today*, becoming the unexpected US Open champion, beating Hingis in the finals and turning heads for powering the tennis ball in volleys as hard as anyone in the game, even her sister.

Midway through the finals match, Serena belted a forehand winner past Hingis with such force that tennis great John McEnroe, sitting in the commentary booth, could only say: "Excuse me?!"

With the win, Serena became the second African

American woman after Althea Gibson in 1958 to win a Grand Slam singles tournament. Playing together, the Williams sisters also won the US Open doubles title, another sign of their ascendance in the tennis world.

Over the next few years, the sisters would dominate the game, more than fulfilling the expectations of their father. During one stretch, Venus won *thirty-five* consecutive singles matches as well as six tournaments, including Wimbledon and the US Open several times. In 2002, Venus became the world's top-ranked female player. She also won the gold medal in the 2000 Olympic Games in Sydney, Australia. During this period, Venus battled tendinitis in her knee and wrists as well as anemia, a blood condition that often causes weariness. Meanwhile, Serena emerged as a top-10 player and won major tournaments, including the US Open.

In 2001, playing in the Indian Wells Masters in the desert in super-hot Palm Springs, California, Venus came down with heat exhaustion. She was so dehydrated she began to cramp, feeling severe pain. Venus's knee also throbbed with pain. Fans couldn't tell, but she even had trouble breathing when she came off the court after a quarterfinals victory over Elena Dementieva.

In the semifinals, Venus was scheduled to face Serena in a much-anticipated match. But Venus told tournament officials she just couldn't go on, her body was in terrible pain. Aware that the big crowd was eager to see the matchup, the officials didn't take Venus's complaints seriously, however. Some wondered if Venus was trying to get out of a match against her sister. The officials kept stalling, hoping Venus would feel better and the match would go on. Finally, they told the fans the truth—Venus wasn't in the right condition to play and Serena would be awarded the victory.

The crowd was incensed. When Serena arrived at the court to play a strong Belgian player named Kim Clijsters in the finals, boos rained down from the stands, something that almost never happens in tennis. Some fans directed loud, disgusting insults at Serena.

"I heard the word nigger a couple of times," Serena writes in her book. "I couldn't believe it . . . I tried to block it out but it's tough to ignore fourteen thousand screaming people—especially when they're screaming at you!"

Serena wanted to cry but held back tears so the cruel fans wouldn't get satisfaction from knowing they had affected her.

As the match began, fans continued screaming at Serena while cheering for Clijsters. At one point, while resting during a changeover, Serena was so emotionally drained she cried into her towel.

She quickly recovered. Bracing herself, she became determined to persevere. *Okay, Serena, you need to be tough*, she thought to herself.

"If Althea Gibson could fight her way through far worse, I had an obligation to fight through this," Serena says, referring to the trailblazing African American tennis star.

Back in action, Serena double-faulted, a huge miscue that gave the crowd more reason to root against her. Somehow, Serena managed to maintain her composure, though. Then a supportive fan screamed out: "Come on, Serena, you can do it!" A few others also began to cheer for Serena, impressed by her courage in the face of the hostile crowd. They lifted Serena's spirits as she realized that some fans were on her side. Somehow, Serena battled back and scored an improbable victory, winning two of three sets, 4–6, 6–4, 6–2.

In the postmatch press conference, Serena was determined to behave in a more dignified way than the fans had behaved.

"To those of you who didn't cheer," Serena said, "I love you anyway."

"I would not be reduced by these people," Serena writes in her book. "I would rise above them."

After Serena's win, the Williams sisters boycotted the Indian Wells tournament for many years, a sign that they hadn't forgotten how they had been treated.

Starting around 2002, Serena's dominance truly began. At Wimbledon, Serena defeated her sister, who had been the top seed in the tournament, to become the world's number-one-ranked female player. The next year, Serena became only the fifth woman ever to hold all four Grand Slam titles simultaneously. She went on to win multiple tournaments and Grand Slam titles over the next few years, reigning over rivals for most of that period thanks to an unmatched baseline game, powerful serves, and remarkable perseverance.

Soon, though, Venus and Serena would be tested in very troubling ways.

In March 2011, Serena was on her way to a party after the Oscar awards when she began having trouble breathing and was rushed to the hospital.

Serena worried a doctor would walk in and tell her she'd have to stop playing tennis. She was actually in more danger than she realized. Tests revealed she had a pulmonary embolism—a potentially fatal blockage in an artery of her lung. Had she waited a couple of days to go to the hospital, Serena would have been in mortal danger. If left untreated, 30 percent of patients die from pulmonary embolisms, according to the Centers for Disease Control and Prevention.

Doctors performed surgery on Serena and she had to endure a difficult recovery.

"It got to the stage where it felt like I could hardly

breathe. Some days I didn't get out of bed at all," she later told the *Guardian*. "I just laid on a couch thinking why has this happened to me."

Serena says recovering from the embolism was hard, but it gave her useful perspective in life, reminding her to appreciate each day. At the time, doctors said the embolism could affect Serena's ability to breathe and make her more susceptible to bruising and bleeding, but as she slowly recovered she vowed to become a champion once again.

After about a year of healing, Serena returned to the court, wowing those same doctors.

Coincidentally, also around the beginning of 2011, Venus began noticing something worrisome happening to her own body. She woke up bone tired and couldn't seem to shake the fatigue the rest of the day.

Venus was just thirty-three at the time. And she was a world-class athlete. It didn't make sense that she had so little energy. Venus and her family began to worry that she had a serious disease. She had trouble just getting out of bed and began blaming herself for not having more energy and motivation.

Am I just lazy? Venus asked herself.

"[At the time] I could never, ever get in shape and I couldn't understand why," Venus says. "It was very difficult."

After months of tests and doctor visits, Venus was diagnosed with Sjögren's syndrome, a debilitating autoimmune disease more common in women than men that afflicts four million Americans. In some ways, the diagnosis was good news for Venus and her family. They had worried she might have a serious disease, maybe one that was life-threatening. It was a relief to finally know what the problem was.

But Sjögren's syndrome can cause joint pain, fatigue, dry eyes, and dry mouth. Worst of all, it's incurable. Soon, Venus was forced to quit the tennis tour and saw her ranking fall to a lowly 103 in the world.

"Not being able to practice has most definitely affected my game," she told a reporter at the time. "I can't get all those extra little things you need, and it's hard to get motivated if you don't feel well, too."

By 2014, Venus was rebuilding her career, winning

tournaments and climbing the rankings. She was a thirty-four-year-old, seven-time Grand Slam champion who will go down in history as among the greatest tennis players ever, but Venus realized her battle with Sjögren's was the toughest in her life and she needed to dig deep and adopt a new attitude—in terms of both the game she loved and her life.

"My motto now is that it all adds up, so if I can only do a little bit this day, it will add up, and it's better than if I get discouraged and don't do anything," she told CNN. "That's when I really start sliding downhill."

In the summer of 2016, Venus and Serena flew to London to compete at Wimbledon, another of the four Grand Slam tournaments. They each had overcome so much, but skeptics doubted their chances of success in the prestigious competition. Venus was coming off a comeback year highlighted by three titles, finishing 2015 ranked in the top ten for the first time in six years. Still, at age thirty-six, Venus was positively ancient in the world of tennis. Serena, at thirty-five, was coming off a losing streak, and, like her sister, some thought she was also too old to be a champion.

Venus managed to beat her first two opponents. In the third round, her age was put to the test as she went up against nineteen-year-old Daria Kasatkina, a player born just before Venus played her first Wimbledon in 1997. The veteran managed to outlast Kasatkina, winning in a third-set tiebreaker to advance. Venus continued to win and went on a surprising run, reaching the semifinals before losing to the fourth-ranked player in the world, Angelique Kerber.

Venus would not go home empty-handed. The Williams sisters won the doubles title and Venus improved her individual ranking to number six in the world, reestablishing herself as a tennis star.

Meanwhile, Serena was dominant throughout the tournament, advancing easily to the singles championship round. In the Wimbledon finals against Angelique Kerber, at a key moment in the match, the score was 3–3 in the second set, with Serena serving, and Kerber had break point, when Serena sent a 117-mile-per-hour serve past Kerber's backhand side, stunning the crowd. A few moments later, Serena dialed it up further, sending a 124-mile-per-hour serve past Kerber. The explosive serves were turning points in the match, helping Serena capture her seventh Wimbledon championship and her twenty-second victory in a major tennis tournament.

In early 2017, Serena beat Venus 6–4, 6–4 to win the Australian Open. For Venus, it was her first major final since 2009, a sign she was still one of the best players in the world, while Serena set an Open-era record for the most Grand Slam titles won by an individual and was again the world's top-ranked female.

After Serena beat Elena Vesnina in the semifinals of the 2016 Wimbledon tournament, she was asked in a post-match press conference if she now should be considered "one of the greatest female athletes of all time."

The question reflected Serena's historic accomplishments. But something seemed to bother Serena, who used the opportunity to make an important point about the value of female athletes.

"I prefer the words 'one of the greatest athletes of all time,'" Serena responded.

Indeed, Serena already had recorded a remarkable accomplishment—at thirty-four she was the oldest player in the Open era to hold the number one ranking, female *or* male.

Serena's point was clear: Gender shouldn't define how women are valued or appreciated. A woman shouldn't be considered a great athlete *for a woman*. She should be viewed as a great athlete. That can be said of female athletes as well as of female doctors, lawyers, and others who excel in life, even those who never pick up a racquet, ball, or glove.

Yet even today, women are often discriminated against, especially in the workplace, with many women still receiving substantially less money than men for doing the same jobs. Fed up with this inequality, Serena has become an important face in the movement for equal pay for men and women.

Once, when Serena was asked about her frequent calls for equal pay and treatment for male and female athletes, she said she would like to "see people, the public, the press, other athletes in general, just realize and respect women for who they are and what we are and what we do."

All champions enjoy lifting trophies over their heads as crowds cheer. But in some ways, Serena and Venus say they've derived so much pleasure from those moments because of the struggles they've weathered.

"Only I know the challenges I've overcome and the long path I've been on," Venus says, referring to dealing with Sjögren's syndrome and other issues.

Venus, who has won seven Grand Slam singles titles and four Olympic gold medals and held the number one world ranking on three separate occasions, says there's only one way to conquer obstacles, find success in life, and become a leader: Identify a sport, hobby, academic interest, or something else you love and are good at, and then put maximum effort into improving each day.

"Following your dreams and tapping into your passion will always lead you to personal success and ultimately happiness," Venus says.

Just make sure to ignore the inevitable doubters

and skeptics, and listen to parents, coaches, and others who support you and provide guidance on ways you can achieve greatness.

"Don't let outsiders bring negativity into your mind and your life," Venus says.

With that message in mind, Venus is setting her sights on the 2020 Olympics, when she'll be forty. Venus says she wants to represent the US once more, because playing in the Olympics is what has made her happiest in her career.

"Stay true to yourself and do something *you* love," Venus says. "And know you *can* go beyond where you think you can go, and it's worth it. Never give up."

As kids, with the encouragement of their father, the Williams sisters set out on a journey to become tennis stars. They had the passion, the drive to excel, and most important of all—a dream. Today, that dream has become a reality as the Williams sisters will go down in history as two of the greatest athletes—female or male—of all time.

MO'NE DAVIS

For many years, girls were ridiculed for their abilities on the baseball field. They were too small, too weak, and too slow and could never compete with boys, skeptics said.

During the summer of 2014, however, the unlikely exploits of a thirteen-year-old named Mo'ne Davis helped change the perception of fans, baseball experts, and others, likely for good.

Growing up in South Philadelphia, Mo'ne had little interest in dolls, art, or dance classes. She was a born athlete who was happiest playing almost any kind of sport.

Mo'ne wasn't a baseball prodigy, though, and never aimed to be any kind of pioneer for other young women.

Early on, she didn't even like baseball very much, preferring basketball or other sports. In fact, when she played baseball she often struggled.

"I usually swung and missed on a tee," Mo'ne says. "Not a lot of people threw to me because I couldn't catch or throw; it was a little embarrassing."

In 2008, when Mo'ne was seven, she was playing football with her cousins and older brother one day when Steve Bandura, the program director at the Marian Anderson Recreation Center in South Philadelphia, walked by the field.

Watching Mo'ne effortlessly throw a football with a perfect spiral, run hard, and tackle the boys, Coach Bandura was instantly impressed with her athleticism. Coach Bandura asked Mo'ne to join a basketball practice at the center. Mo'ne agreed, and when she showed up at practice, she watched as the boys, including her older cousin, tried to keep up with a complicated "three-man weave" basketball drill. Within minutes, Mo'ne, the only girl on the court, joined in on the action.

"She went through it like she had been doing it a

thousand times," an impressed Bandura later told the *Philadelphia Tribune*.

Mo'ne fit in so well that Coach Bandura invited her to become a member of the team, which also played soccer and baseball in local leagues. But Mo'ne's mother, Lakeisha McLean, vetoed the idea.

"When she found out it was all boys, Mom didn't want me to play," Mo'ne says. "She was afraid I'd get hurt, she kept saying no. She was not happy about it."

Mo'ne was persistent, however, asking her mother for permission on an almost daily basis. She couldn't forget the fun she had playing with the team and wanted more.

"I'll be *fine*," Mo'ne insisted to her mother.

Eventually, her mother gave in and let Mo'ne join Coach Bandura's team.

"I wore her down," Mo'ne says. "I just really wanted to play, I just wanted to try something new."

Soon, Mo'ne wasn't just the team's only female member, she also was one of its best players. But when she played rival squads in various sports, Mo'ne often heard skepticism or even mockery from opposing players.

"Guys were thinking they were stronger and faster in soccer, so whenever I did something good [on the field] they gave a shocked look. It was the coolest thing ever," Mo'ne says.

Sometimes, even parents of rival teams made negative comments about how the lone girl on the field wouldn't be able to keep up with the boys.

"A lot of parents trash talked on the side," she says. "I heard it but didn't pay any attention or I'd start laughing, to show them I didn't really care . . . whatever they said was just funny [to me]."

Mo'ne played a variety of sports for Coach Bandura, including baseball, but basketball remained Mo'ne's favorite. In fact, she almost quit baseball at age nine.

"I wasn't really into baseball until I was nine or ten," she says. "I wasn't the best on the team, I was just another player."

When playing baseball, Mo'ne usually was an outfielder. One day, though, Coach Bandura, perhaps remembering Mo'ne's impressive football-throwing ability, asked her if she wanted to pitch. From the start, Mo'ne had impressive control and accuracy, but she didn't have much velocity. The coach said he didn't mind.

"Throw strikes," he told her. "Let your teammates field the ball."

The Anderson Monarchs practiced almost daily and Mo'ne kept working on her pitching mechanics. Over time, she began to throw much harder, impressing her coach and teammates.

"Somehow my arm got stronger," Mo'ne says. "Coach Steve said I had a good arm so I kept coming to practice to improve."

Back at school, Mo'ne's friends were supportive of her sports ambitions, saying it was cool she was playing with boys. That bolstered Mo'ne's confidence. But some were worried for her, just like Mo'ne's mother had been.

"Aren't you scared of getting hurt?" a friend asked.

Mo'ne reassured her that she would be fine.

As the Monarchs' starting pitcher, Mo'ne didn't hide the fact that she was the only girl on the team. She even wore a distinctive, hot-pink baseball glove. It was Mo'ne's favorite color at the time and the glove had been a present from her mother, so Mo'ne wasn't going to hide it or choose a different color. She was comfortable being herself, even if she began to draw attention.

"The first time we played [the Monarchs] I remember looking and wondering why this baseman had a pink glove," said Jesse Balcer, coach of the Fox Rox Baseball Club, which played against Mo'ne's team. "Then I looked closer and thought, wait a minute, that's not a boy, it's a girl!"

One time, as Mo'ne walked out to the mound at the Marian Anderson Recreation Center, she heard the opposing team laughing at her and her glove.

"We're gonna kill them!" Mo'ne remembers them saying. "There's a girl pitching!"

Mo'ne just looked at her teammates and smiled. By then, she was consistently throwing a fastball that topped 60 miles per hour. She knew the boys should have been nervous, not cocky, about facing her. The teasing made Mo'ne even more determined to succeed.

"I was ready to go out there and shut them down," she says.

Mo'ne says she pitched a shutout, leading her team to victory.

Other outings were rougher. In one game when she was around eleven years old, Mo'ne pitched against an aptly named team called the Bombers. Facing a lineup stacked with tough hitters, she was pounded, giving up four home runs in a single inning.

"It was the worst day," she says. "I just kept throwing strikes and somehow I got out of the inning."

Afterward, Mo'ne says she tried to keep her confidence up, reminding herself that even major league pitching stars have bad days.

"I was disappointed because I let my team down, but I told myself this was going to happen at some point," she says.

Around 2011, at age ten, Mo'ne says she realized she was emerging as a dominant player. In tournament games against top-seeded teams, Mo'ne usually was given the start, a clear recognition that she was her team's best pitcher.

"I was like, 'Oh my, I didn't know I could pitch like this,'" she says. "I was good, though I knew there was still room for improvement."

Mo'ne's reputation began to spread and opponents

took notice. Before long, no one was laughing at Mo'ne or the color of her glove.

Skill, training, and discipline were the keys to her developing talent. Mo'ne had to sacrifice for her love of the game. She took a bus at 6:15 a.m. each morning to travel to school. After school, she would go to the recreational center for practice or games. Her work ethic was just as impressive as her ability to dominate the boys, who were as big as six foot three, in her Philadelphia league.

In 2014, Mo'ne and a Philadelphia team she had joined, the Taney Dragons, set out to try to make the Little League World Series (LLWS). In a qualifying game in August of that year, Mo'ne, now thirteen years old, was the starting pitcher and she threw a three-hit, complete game shutout to qualify the Dragons for the LLWS in South Williamsport, Pennsylvania, where the world would be watching. By then, Mo'ne had garnered her share of publicity, including articles in local newspapers.

She wasn't prepared for what was ahead, however.

• • •

From the first game in the World Series, all eyes were on Mo'ne. It wasn't just that she was the first African American girl to compete in tournament history or that she was one of just eighteen female players in LLWS history—fans and analysts were simply in awe of her incredible talent.

Throwing with a compact, over-the-top motion, falling slightly to her left with a style that some compared to former Boston Red Sox star closer Jonathan Papelbon, Mo'ne dominated from the opening game's first inning. Though she later acknowledged dealing with nerves, few in the stands could tell. Mo'ne's fastball reached 70 miles per hour and her curveball hit the exact spots where she'd aimed, as she began mowing down opposing hitters from the team from South Nashville, Tennessee.

By the fifth inning, Mo'ne had only thrown forty-four pitches and seemed fresh and in control, while Nashville's starter had already reached the eighty-five-pitch Little League limit. In the sixth and final inning, Mo'ne struck out the first two batters. The third made it to a full count, three balls and two strikes, but

Mo'ne struck him out, too, finishing off the victory.

In all, Mo'ne had struck out eight batters and allowed no walks and only two hits in the complete game 4–0 shutout victory, her second complete game in a row. With the win, Mo'ne etched her name in the record books by becoming the first girl to toss a shutout in LLWS history.

The performance astounded fans in attendance and those watching on TV. Some began to look up to Mo'ne. In the stands, a young girl on her father's shoulders held a handmade sign up high: "I want to throw like a girl!" The photo was featured in newspapers and shared online and on social media, further evidence of the inspiration Mo'ne was giving to so many, even adults.

"The 13-year-old baseball sensation has emerged as one of the best sports stories of the summer," columnist Jason Gay wrote in the *Wall Street Journal.* "It was a calm, dominant performance . . . it's hard to not be moved by the excitement created by the right-handed ace."

Even major leaguers took notice. American League

MVP Mike Trout saluted her on Twitter: "Mo'ne Davis is straight dominating . . . fun to watch!!!"

Boston Red Sox slugger David Ortiz told ESPN that Mo'ne "throws serious cheese," referring to her fastball.

Praise poured in from other celebrities and athletes like TV show host Ellen DeGeneres, basketball star Kevin Durant, legendary tennis player Billie Jean King, First Lady Michelle Obama and many others. Mo'ne's story captivated the nation because it demonstrated that girls can accomplish any goal they set out for themselves, even on a playing field usually dominated by boys.

"It was the coolest thing ever," Mo'ne says. "I don't think many of these people actually had watched the Little League World series before. It was very overwhelming."

Even as the nation cheered her performance, though, Mo'ne appeared calm and composed. In interviews, she usually gave confident answers, often laced with sly humor.

"I throw my curveball like Clayton Kershaw," she said in one interview, referring to the Los Angeles

Dodgers' flamethrower, "and my fastball like Mo'ne Davis."

Asked by ESPN whether she minded all the new-found attention and interview requests pouring in from all over the world, she had a perfect answer.

"I can always say no," Mo'ne said.

In her next start, Mo'ne wasn't quite as dominant, though she struck out six batters in just over two innings of work in her team's 8–1 loss to a Nevada team considered the best hitting squad in the tournament.

"Everyone knew their lineup was stacked with great players," Mo'ne says. "I went in very nervous but somehow the nerves went away."

In their next game, a do-or-die match against a squad from Chicago, Mo'ne and her Philadelphia team were down by four runs early in the game. But they fought back, cutting down their opponent's lead to one run. Unfortunately, that was as close as they would come. They lost the game and Mo'ne and her teammates were knocked out of the tournament, but the sports world was still buzzing about all she had accomplished and the impact she was having.

That week, Mo'ne became the first Little League baseball player to appear on the cover of *Sports Illustrated*. Later, she earned the Associated Press's Female Athlete of the Year award. Mo'ne even helped inspire a 2016 television show called *Pitch*, about a female pitcher with a chance to the play in the major leagues, a sign of her wider impact on society.

Mo'ne's talent and tenacity helped change the perceptions many had of female athletes, and she even became a role model, something Mo'ne says made her proud.

After the tournament, "a lot of girls say they began trying out" for new sports, Mo'ne says. "I like that I had an opportunity to show we girls can hang with the guys."

Mo'ne couldn't return to the LLWS after her 2014 feat because she was past the tournament's age limit. She continued to play summer ball for the Anderson Monarchs, though. And her success forced fans and baseball experts to consider the possibility that a female player could emerge as a star in the major leagues at some point in the years ahead.

In fact, in 2015, Melissa Mayeux, a sixteen-year-old French shortstop, garnered attention when she became the first female player added to Major League Baseball's international registration list, making her eligible to be signed by an MLB club.

"Davis captivated America," the *Washington Post* wrote. "Thanks to the performances of Davis and Mayeux . . . the wait for fiction to turn into reality is dwindling."

In the years since her historic performance at the 2014 LLWS, Mo'ne has continued to play a variety of sports against boys, enjoying each.

"Winning is winning," she says. "I just enjoy the opportunity to get better."

As a tenth grader, she mostly plays baseball, soccer, and basketball today, but she's decided on a new goal: playing college basketball and then advancing to the WNBA.

Despite her amazing accomplishments, from time to time, she still hears trash talk from rivals or parents on the sidelines.

"It's not every game, just whenever we're beating

a team and parents start getting mad," Mo'ne says.

Mo'ne has a piece of advice for other girls in similar situations: Ignore the skeptics and those who share insults, not inspiration.

"There always will be people who will put you down or try to hurt you," she says. "Just know that life won't always be an uphill arrow, there are some bumps and obstacles, just keep pushing and working hard and staying in school and you will see the hard work rewarded."

BETHANY HAMILTON

Sometimes it's easy to predict how a physical difference or other challenge will serve as an imposing obstacle in life. Other times, however, setbacks arrive unexpectedly. These can be the most difficult challenges one could possibly face because they emerge abruptly, providing no time to prepare or adjust.

As a young teenager, Bethany Hamilton suffered a tragedy that was sudden and shocking. She was so devastated even her family and friends expected Bethany to abandon her life's dream.

But Bethany wasn't willing to give up.

• • •

From an early age, Bethany had a single passion: surfing. Bethany had fun playing soccer and other sports, but there was something different about surfing—for her, the sport is "a pleasure rush indescribable to anyone who has not experienced it."

Bethany lived in Hawaii and began hitting the waves at the age of five, guided by her parents, Tom and Cheri. She was a natural in the water, and at age seven, Bethany could surf and catch waves without any help, winning her first competition on the island of Oahu just a year later.

"My passion for surfing ignited and went off," says Bethany.

Bethany's family wasn't wealthy, but her parents managed to pay for contest entrance fees, car rentals, and other transportation costs. Most important, her parents gave Bethany their full support as she chased her dream.

"My parents were able to get me a surfboard and get me to the beach, and that's all I needed," she says. "My mom and dad weren't financially well off but they provided the best they could and always cheered for me."

When Bethany began to participate in more serious amateur surfing competitions, it became clear she had a great deal of talent. In 2002, she won the explorer women's division of the National Scholastic Surfing Association's (NSSA) Open and Explorer event on Kauai. It was her first win at a major amateur contest. Yet Bethany was no stranger to success. Even before the NSSA competition, she beat out older surfers to win the women's division at a contest at Ala Moana on Oahu.

Beyond her obvious talent, discipline and training were key to Bethany's early success. She worked hard on her physical condition, which in turn helped her surfing. But after watching competitors carefully, Bethany came to realize she'd require something else to reach the ambitious goals she was setting for herself in surfing. She also needed a strong mental approach to the sport.

Rivals were often intimidated when they saw a huge wave rushing toward them, but Bethany would steady her nerves and try to stay confident. When she traveled to compete in a spot where she had never surfed, Bethany worked hard to stay calm and not let local girls more familiar with the area beat her.

"What separates the best from the rest is the ability to overcome hard stuff," Bethany says. "The ocean is always challenging; it's frustrating at times and your ability to adapt and adjust to changing conditions is crucial."

Bethany's ability to stay cool under pressure would serve her well later in life.

By age thirteen, Bethany seemed to have a bright future. She was a top amateur surfer with a loving and supportive family. Some thought she might even be gifted enough to become a professional surfer. Bethany was dedicated to doing everything she could to pursue her dream.

Then came the terrifying morning that would change everything.

Early on October 31, 2003—Halloween morning— Bethany's mother, Cheri, opened Bethany's bedroom door a crack to ask a question: "Wanna go surfing?"

Within minutes, Bethany was out of bed and dressed for the beach. It was still dark when they headed for a spot on the north shore of Kauai. The waves were too calm, though, and Bethany and her mother were about to drive home when Bethany suggested they check out nearby Tunnels Beach. The waves there weren't much more exciting, but Bethany spotted a friend, Alana Blanchard, and asked if she could stay. Bethany waved good-bye to her mother and paddled out with Alana.

Unable to find challenging waves, Bethany relaxed on her surfboard, her left hand dangling in the cool blue ocean. The crystal-clear water was as peaceful and calm as a backyard swimming pool.

"I had no warning at all, not even the slightest hint of danger on the horizon," she says.

Out of nowhere, Bethany saw a flash of gray. A split second later, she felt two lightning-fast tugs and then tremendous pressure on her left side. Bethany saw the jaws of a huge, fourteen-foot tiger shark covering the top of the surfboard and her entire left arm. Almost immediately, the water around her turned bright red.

Bethany realized her left arm was gone, almost to the armpit.

"It was over in a few seconds . . . There was no pain," Bethany writes in her book. "I felt pressure and kind of a jiggle-jiggle tug, which I know now was the teeth."

Somehow calm, perhaps because she was in a daze, Bethany began furiously paddling back to the beach, relying on her right arm and getting help from Alana and others who saw the attack. Onshore, Alana's father, Holt Blanchard, reacted quickly, wrapping a T-shirt and a surfboard leash around the area of the wound to serve as a tourniquet and stop the bleeding.

He likely saved Bethany's life. But she had lost 60 percent of her blood in the attack and kept passing out as paramedics raced her to the hospital. Soon she would be in surgery as doctors struggled to keep her alive.

Surfers sometimes face dangers from sharks. In 2015, a top men's competitive event in South Africa was canceled after a three-time world champion surfer fought off a shark, punching it and swimming to safety. But shark attacks rarely happen, underscoring how shocked Bethany's family was when they heard about the accident.

The surgeries went well and her doctors were thrilled with her progress and confident she'd be released from the hospital within a week or two. Because she kept herself in top condition, Bethany was better able to survive the huge blood loss, doctors said.

She was shaken by the attack, though. As she recovered, Bethany had early doubts about her future.

"I put on a brave face for everyone, but I can't pretend it didn't get to me at times," Bethany says.

The early challenges were imposing. Bethany suffered some lasting pain from the injury. And she knew she would have to deal with the physical challenge of leading a life with only one arm and relearning to do even simple things, such as tie her shoelaces and put on a shirt.

Bethany also experienced mental anguish. Her life was devoted to surfing and, before the accident, she had hoped to become a competitive surfer. Now her dreams seemed dashed and she didn't know how to handle the sudden change.

"There was pain, doubt, and fear," she says. "The mental side of things was the hardest part, though physically difficult, too, it was all intertwined . . . All these feelings flooded into my head, it was incredibly hard, I didn't know what I would be capable of."

Bethany's family and friends shared her concerns. Her father told a local television station that he wasn't sure if she would continue surfing. Bethany started to consider pursuing other activities. She told her parents she'd like to be a surf photographer and mentioned to a friend that she'd get back into soccer.

"For a while I doubted I would ever surf again," she writes in her book.

One day, Bethany met one of her older brother's friends who had lost a leg to a shark five years earlier and eventually resumed surfing. *If he could do it, maybe I could*, Bethany thought.

"He was my first hint of hope," Bethany says. "I began to think that maybe I could surf with one arm. I was willing to try."

In some ways, she says, surfing had prepared her for the challenges she knew were ahead.

"It's a battle and you have to adjust; surfers really have to be resilient . . . now it would be that much more challenging."

Bethany says her religious faith also helped her. She felt God had a plan for her and was guiding her and helping her adjust to living with only one arm. Members of her church came to her hospital room and helped cheer her up.

"I was grounded in faith and that gave me hope," she says.

Before long, Bethany had come to a decision: She would try to resume her surfing career.

"I don't think I could handle not chasing my dream," she says.

It took months for Bethany to adjust to having just one arm. An occupational therapist taught her how to tie her shoelaces with one hand, get dressed, and take care of herself. The last thing Bethany wanted was the pity of others, so she persevered. At home, though, when the bandages came off and she looked at her stump of an arm for the first time, she almost fainted.

I look like a monster, she remembers thinking.

But Bethany appreciated the fact that she had survived the attack and was healthy in every other way. There was an outpouring of support from around the world from people who had heard about the attack and were amazed by her upbeat attitude. Bethany even appeared on various television shows. Support from Bethany's family, friends, and community gave her encouragement.

The question remained, however: Would she be scared to go back into the ocean? And would she be able to surf?

About a month after leaving the hospital, Bethany agreed to watch some friends surf. Once she arrived at the beach, she decided to try to get back on her surfboard. Bethany was nervous but tried to ignore her nagging self-doubt.

She walked into the surf with her friend Alana and didn't even think about being attacked again. Instead,

Bethany focused on the task at hand, attempting to figure out how to paddle with just one arm. On her first couple of tries, she couldn't get up on the board, which was very discouraging.

Bethany refused to give up.

Then it happened. Bethany managed to balance herself on the board, caught a wave, and began surfing. Tears of joy trickled down her face.

"It's hard for me to describe the joy I felt," Bethany says.

Over the next year, Bethany continued to learn to adjust to her new circumstances and became more comfortable on the board. In many ways, she was learning how to surf all over again. But this time she had to deal with certain restrictions. Instead of paddling with two arms, Bethany learned a more effective way to propel herself by kicking hard with her feet. She and her coach placed a hand strap in the top center of her board so she could grab hold with her right hand and push the board underwater. She had a lifelike prosthetic arm custom made for her, but she almost never used it.

Her courage inspired young people and adults alike all over the world.

In July 2004, Bethany entered the national championship of the NSSA in Huntington Beach, California. She didn't win but she earned the respect of fans, including actor Adam Sandler, as well as fellow competitors.

"One arm or not, this girl proved she's back in the saddle and will be a nationals contender for years to come," wrote Janice Aragon, a blogger for the surfing association.

Indeed, over the next few years, Bethany either won or came close to winning various events, capturing her first national amateur title in 2005 before turning professional in 2007. Since then she has participated in numerous Association of Surfing Professionals and World Tour events, taking second place at the 2009 World Junior Championships.

In the spring of 2016, when Bethany was twenty-six, she was given a wild card berth in an event hosted by the elite World Surf League in a competition in Fiji. The contest didn't start well. In the first-round group,

Bethany finished last, which confirmed to skeptics that her invitation had merely been a publicity stunt, not a recognition of her abilities.

Bethany would have to win a second-chance heat to remain in the competition. She was up against Tyler Wright, the world's number one female surfer and a six-time world champion.

Bethany's first ride was scored 7.1 out of 10, a solid but unremarkable result. But her second ride was a thing of beauty. Bethany started with a quick tube ride under the curl of a wave before executing four slashing turns that wowed the crowd, scoring an impressive 9.0 on the run. Her combined 16.1 topped Wright's 14.9, a shocking upset. Bethany went on to win the third round as well as the quarterfinals. She was eliminated in the semifinals, finishing third overall, but it was Bethany's best competitive result in her career.

Experts were amazed. "Few expected Hamilton to reach the top level of the sport while surfing with just one arm," the *New York Times* wrote that day.

"I knew once I beat Tyler I could beat anyone,"

Bethany told an interviewer after reaching the quarterfinals. "At the end of the day, it's just putting it together and catching the right waves and surfing my best."

It was a sign Bethany was continuing to improve, adapt, and persevere. Bethany, who saw her life story hit the silver screen in 2011 in the movie *Soul Surfer*, acknowledges that she's been able to turn tragedy into triumph.

Through promotions, television appearances, competitions, and marketing, she managed to earn a substantial salary. "I was lucky enough to travel around the world several times before I was even an adult," Bethany acknowledges.

But she continues to face difficulties. "Coping with people's stares . . . answering endless questions . . . learning to [deal] with the frustration of knowing that if I had both arms to paddle, I just might have done a little better in a surf contest," she writes.

Bethany continues to overcome the obstacles thrown her way, allowing her to live a rewarding life. In 2015, Bethany and her husband welcomed a healthy baby boy named Tobias. Bethany was thrilled, of course, but also anxious about how she would manage to deal with a squirming baby.

"What I don't want is for people to pity me or think of me as a person who has had her life ruined," she writes. "It's my reality now, I've learned to accept it. I've moved on."

Bethany says everyone will face battles at some point in their lives.

"We all have sudden struggles," Bethany says. "When hard times come our way, how will we react and what will we fight for?"

Just as she wasn't ready to give up on surfing, Bethany's advice is to cling tight to one's passions when faced with an unexpected challenge.

"I look at the loss of my arm and say, 'Wow, so much good has come out of it, it's worth it in a weird way,'" she says. "Life is so much more than your ambition and goals, it's about giving back to the community and the next generation, and cheering them and their talents."

Bethany made progress when she realized that her

fears were holding her back, not her missing limb. It's a lesson she says can be helpful for others. "So often we're held back by fears of the unknown. If something is uncomfortable or challenging we don't want to give it a chance."

It's understandable to have self-doubt and nervousness about life's challenges. Face your fears and don't let them stop you, Bethany says. Things may work out better than one could ever imagine.

CARLI LLOYD

After 120 grueling minutes of play, the score remained tied at 2–2. The final match in the 2011 Women's World Cup would come down to penalty kicks to decide the winner. A palpable tension filled the stadium as the US and Japanese soccer teams retreated to their benches to prepare for the shootout. Carli Lloyd and her American teammates felt the pressure building.

The US team had endured a difficult journey to get to the finals. They were nearly knocked out in a quarterfinals match against Brazil, surviving after tying the match in the 122nd minute and then winning on penalty kicks in one of most riveting games in the history of the Women's World Cup.

It had been twelve years since the US Women's National Team had reached the finals. Carli knew a single goal could make the difference. She had been benched during early matches of the World Cup but she knew this was the perfect opportunity to solidify her spot on the team and become an instant legend.

Carli prepared for her shot, deciding on a strategy.

"All these mixed emotions are going through your head," she says.

Does the goalkeeper know where you're going? Do you hit it harder or softer?

Focused, Carli approached the ball hard and blasted a powerful shot toward the middle of the goal. The goalkeeper dove to her right, leaving an opening close to the top of the goal, exactly where Carli was aiming. For a moment, it looked like her shot would find net and Carli would be a hero.

Glancing up, however, Carli watched in horror as the ball soared high over the crossbar, badly missing its target. Carli stared ahead, almost in disbelief, cupped her mouth with her left hand, and quietly walked back to join her teammates. The US Women's National

Team had lost to Japan, extending their trophy drought.

For days, Carli was dejected and depressed.

"It was a really tough thing to go through," she said. "I felt kind of like a failure, felt like I let the team down . . . I was pretty devastated."

It was the lowest moment of Carli's life, an experience that would have completely demoralized many players and even ended some careers.

Somehow, Carli would have to find a way to turn this major setback into something more positive.

Growing up in Delran Township, a small town in southern New Jersey, Carli began playing soccer at age five, developing an early love of the sport, constantly working on her game at a field near her home. Carli would practice shot after shot, often on her own. Before long, Carli emerged as perhaps the best young player in the state.

A five-foot-eight midfielder, Carli won two New Jersey State Cups playing for the Medford Strikers Soccer Club and scored twenty-six goals during her senior year in high school as captain of her varsity team, distinguishing herself with superb ball control and dribbling skills, essential traits for an attacking midfielder.

In some ways, soccer came *too* easily to Carli. Growing up, she usually was the best player on her teams, relying on raw, natural ability. Carli received a scholarship to attend Rutgers University and excelled from her first game, starting every match her freshman year and leading the team with fifteen goals. Eventually, she broke the Rutgers scoring records and became a first-team All–Big East choice four straight years.

During her college career, Carli had little need to hone various aspects of her game. She relied on the same skill set she had used to great advantage all her life, playing purely as an attacker, sitting behind the two main strikers with few defensive responsibilities. Carli waited for the ball and had little need for technique. Her offensive game was so strong that coaches and others applauded and congratulated her, rarely asking for more.

After her junior year of college, Carli was selected for the Under-21 Women's National Team, a huge break that opened up the possibility of a professional career. But Carli struggled for the first time in her life. Playing with other talented women, Carli saw that her natural ability was no longer sufficient and she quickly lost confidence. Even worse, Carli blamed her coaches and teammates for her lackluster play.

"When you get to the national team, everybody's that type of player," she told the *Houston Chronicle*. "I couldn't crack through. I just couldn't crack through."

Eventually, Coach Chris Petrucelli, the U-21 coach, cut Carli from the team.

"You're really talented, but there are holes in your game that need to be fixed," Coach Petrucelli told her, referring to her defense and ability to work away from the ball. "You're not ready."

Carli left the room crying. She went home and told her parents that she was going to finish her last year at Rutgers and then quit the sport. Her parents were disappointed after investing so much time and money in their daughter's soccer career and were sad to see her turn her back on a sport that she had been so passionate about.

They encouraged Carli not to give up—hold on a little longer and maybe she could make the senior national team.

"If I can't even make Under-21, how am I gonna make the national team?" Carli responded.

Carli mentally checked out. She spent her final year of college focused on socializing, enjoying college life, and other things she couldn't do before because of the work she'd put into her training and games.

One day in 2003, Carli's father, Stephen, was attending a training session with Carli's brother run by James Galanis, a top coach in the region. Coach Galanis had spent three years playing professional soccer in Australia and previously had been coached by Ferenc Puskas, a Hungarian who was considered one of the greatest players of all time.

Coach Galanis was walking to his car when Stephen approached.

"My daughter needs you," he put simply. "She wants to play for the national team."

Carli had just received news that a player on the U-21 team had been injured and the team's coaches wanted to reevaluate Carli to see if there was any way she could help the team, even in a small role.

Coach Galanis recalled Carli's skills from working with one of her teammates years earlier, but he also remembered the huge flaws in her game. He gave Stephen his number and told him to have Carli call to set up an evaluation.

Carli, still in a funk, took weeks to place the call. When they finally got together and began drills, it was obvious they had a lot of work ahead to get Carli to the point where she could compete for a spot on the national team. In fact, it seemed doubtful she'd ever get to that point. After only twenty minutes of work, Carli was gassed.

Carli was "skilled, had spent time playing with freedom, and had a street savviness and was tactically savvy," Coach Galanis says. But Carli lacked physical fitness and only "worked hard when she wanted to work hard, not all the time."

Carli was a bit of a diva. She had been surrounded

by coaches who used her to help their teams win, but they never pushed her very much to improve.

"I don't think she was being treated like everyone else on the team, because [she was] so skilled," Coach Galanis says. "When she didn't work hard [she] didn't have coaches around her to say that wasn't acceptable . . . Coaches would let her cruise . . . they didn't want to piss her off because she was their star player."

Coach Galanis asked Carli some probing questions.

"Why did you get cut from the team?" he asked.

Carli was full of excuses. "The coach didn't like me [and] the girls were egotistical," she responded.

Coach Galanis wasn't happy with what he heard. Eventually, he sat Carli down for a difficult conversation.

"What do you want to do with your career?" he asked.

"I want to play national for the national team."

"I believe there are five major pillars of [soccer]," he told her. "You have the first two—technical skill and tactical awareness. But you're lacking the last three: work ethic, mental toughness, and 'coachability,'" or good habits on and off the pitch.

"If you can improve your weaknesses and turn them into strengths, then you can become one of the best players in the world," Coach Galanis said.

Carli shot him a look of disbelief. The coach must be joking, Carli thought.

"But this has to be your entire life," Coach Galanis continued. "If I call you on a Saturday night when you are with your friends and I tell you that you need to be at the field in thirty minutes, you say, 'Sorry, guys, I have to go.' This has to come before every-thing . . . boyfriends, friends, family, everything. Unless you have that commitment, I'm not doing this."

She had never gotten this kind of critique or lec-ture from a coach. She needed to hear it. Inspired by her coach's words, Carli decided to devote herself to the sport. It would be a turning point in her life.

In addition to improving Carli's fitness, Coach Galanis worked on her technique and in-game focus. After noticing she didn't strike the ball properly, he even worked on adjusting her shooting form.

Because Coach Galanis was convinced Carli could

achieve greatness, she became willing to make the dramatic changes to her game that he requested.

"It was the first time in my career that I felt that someone believed in me to the point where they could actually get me there," Carli says.

The coach didn't even charge Carli or her parents for his help.

"I had to spend so much time with her that I knew it would cost them a fortune even if I charged them $20 an hour," instead of his usual $100 fee, he says. "I also knew that she really had the potential if she listened and applied herself."

Many of Coach Galanis's friends and even his family thought he was foolish for devoting so much time to someone so headstrong who seemed a long shot to make the national team.

"I said she could be the best player in the world, but they kind of chuckled," Coach Galanis remembers. "They thought I was nuts, even Carli's family."

In 2004, Carli started every game for the U-21 team at that year's Nordic Cup in Iceland, finally earning Coach Petrucelli's faith and emerging as a true star.

The next year, she made the senior US Women's National Team, emerging as an attacking and intimidating midfielder.

Carli's first moment in the national spotlight came in the 2008 Olympics in Beijing during the final match against Brazil. Six minutes into extra time, Carli took a booming, left-footed shot that found net, leading the US team to a gold medal. That year, Carli was named US Soccer Athlete of the Year, along with the US Men's National Team goalie Tim Howard.

Coach Galanis was most proud that Carli had battled for over 90 minutes in the scoreless game without getting discouraged, as she likely would have become just a few years earlier. But even after Carli's team won the gold, her training only became more grueling. Every day she did as many as one thousand sit-ups and five hundred push-ups. Her confidence wasn't yet at the level where it needed to be. To most fans, Carli already was a superstar. But she and her coach knew she hadn't yet reached her full potential. Coach Galanis had faith in her and believed she was getting there, however.

Now we're on our way, he thought.

Then came a major setback: the 2011 World Cup Finals and Carli's embarrassing penalty-kick miscue. For days after the match, she was despondent. Coach Galanis tried to cheer her up, reminding Carli that she'd worked tirelessly for five years to improve and helped the US win Olympic gold along with a number of important tournaments.

"This penalty kick does not represent who you are," he emphasized, reminding Carli how well she had played throughout the World Cup. "Anyone can miss a penalty kick; this won't drag you down . . . just get back to work."

"It was really hard because that's the last impression that people have of you," Carli said at the time, referring to the missed kick. "It starts to play mind games with you, but I missed. I had to get over it."

Within a few days, Carli was training again, with an eye toward winning the 2012 Olympics. Her mind still wasn't fully focused on soccer, however. Days before the Olympics began, after playing a poor half in a pretournament match in Philadelphia, Carli got some shocking news from the US coach—she was being benched for another midfielder, Shannon Boxx. In two short years, Carli had gone from player of the year and Olympic hero to just another backup.

This time, Carli didn't sulk or blame others. She returned home and trained day and night with Coach Galanis.

"I could tell she was hurt, big-time," he says. "But I wanted her to feel the pain" to spur Carli to train even harder.

On the third day of training, the coach walked her back to her car.

"Are you all right?" he asked.

Carli began to cry.

"It sucks, after one bad half, this happens," she said. "It's unfair."

"That's the coach's decision, but we're gonna prove her wrong," Coach Galanis responded. "You'll get time, maybe ten minutes, maybe more, but you're going to have your chance to shine."

His perspective made sense to Carli. She resolved to be a good teammate and to be ready when called upon. Arriving at the Olympics, Carli didn't feel sharp enough. As a backup, she wasn't playing full games and didn't think she was in ideal shape. Some athletes are naturally fit; Carli was someone who needed to work hard to stay in game shape.

On her own, Carli snuck out of the team's dorm rooms at five a.m. to improve her fitness. All alone, she'd sprint on sidewalks, past the front lawns of sleeping locals. She put water bottles on the ground to serve as cones and dribble around them, working on sharp cuts. Carli even got the keys to the stadium and worked on her shooting. She also sprinted up and down the stairs. She no longer needed her coach to motivate her; Carli pushed herself.

Seventeen minutes into the tournament opener against France, Boxx got injured and Carli was called into the game, giving her an early chance for redemption. At the time, the US was down 2–0. Playing with newfound ferocity and focus, Carli helped her team engineer a remarkable comeback, getting the ball outside the box and firing in the game winner to help the US advance.

All her training began to pay off during the rest of the tournament. Carli was in the best shape of her life, even as opponents slowed by the end of the tournament, and she scored both goals in the finals against Japan in the US's 2–1 victory. Carli became the only player in history—man or woman—to score game winners in two separate Olympic gold medal matches.

Carli had discovered the secret to success—intense training, patience, and resilience. She had managed to turn setbacks into successes. Her game continued to improve. The next year, Carli became the highest-scoring midfielder in the history of the US women's team.

In the 2015 World Cup, Carli was named team captain for a number of matches, including the final against Japan, scoring six goals in the tournament. She wore the number ten jersey, the premier number in soccer, one that's usually given to the most gifted and creative attacker.

Carli even scored a hat trick in that year's finals to bring victory to the US, amazing fans and commentators.

"It was the greatest individual performance in a

World Cup final ever," *USA Today* wrote. "I don't care if you're a man or woman. It doesn't matter. Scoring a hat trick in 16 minutes in a final, with the third goal being a shot from half field, that's it. That's the end of discussion."

The last goal was absolutely stunning—a daring 54-yard shot from *midfield* that somehow eluded Japanese goalie Ayumi Kaihori, who found herself just a bit far outside the goal. Reuters called it "one of the most remarkable goals ever witnessed in a Women's World Cup."

As the ball went in, Carli flashed one of the biggest smiles fans had ever seen. Of all those in attendance, Coach Galanis alone realized that for all her success, Carli had only recently developed the confidence necessary to dominate such an important match.

Carli was quick to share credit for her success.

"To be honest, for a number of years, even up until recently, I didn't really have the self-belief in myself," she said that year. "I credit a lot obviously to my trainer back home who took me under his wing. He was the only person in my life who fully believed that I could make the national team. I've gone out and busted my butt."

Much of the explanation for Carli's turnaround also is attributable to her ability to recover and learn from the lows of her life, such as the missed penalty kick.

Looking back, Carli says, "I think that [kind of setback] builds character."

After three dominant tournaments, Carli and the women's national team's success ran out during the 2016 Olympics. They managed to make it out of the group stages but could not break a stalemate in a game against Sweden.

It went to a penalty shoot-out. Carli converted the penalty this time, but it was not enough to clinch a win. The team lost in the quarterfinals.

"You did everything you possibly [could]," Coach Galanis told Carli, trying to console her.

A week after the big loss, Carli called her coach, eager to get back to training. Coach Galanis had to force *her* to take a couple of weeks off. Carli once had been someone with ample skill but little work ethic. Through years of physical and mental training, she improved her attitude and never stopped working until she became one of the best soccer players in the world.

By 2017, Carli was a global superstar who twice had won the FIFA Player of the Year award. At thirty-four, she said she had two last goals before walking away from the sport—the 2019 World Cup and the 2020 Olympics.

Asked how she'd been able to overcome various obstacles in her life, and what advice she'd give others dealing with their own issues, Carli took a few moments to contemplate the question before sharing a crucial lesson for young people.

"You've got to work hard to turn negatives into positives," Carli said. "That's really the key in life."

Carli's lesson is valuable for those competing on the sports field as well as those eager for success elsewhere in life.

WILMA RUDOLPH

No one in their right mind could have predicted that Wilma Rudolph would become an Olympic champion.

For a long time, she could barely walk. Running seemed out of the question.

Wilma was born in 1940 to a poor African American family and grew up in the little town of Clarksville, Tennessee, the twentieth of twenty-two kids. Wilma's father worked as a porter at a railroad station and did odd jobs around town, like painting people's homes, while her mother cleaned the houses of local white families, working six days a week.

Wilma's home lacked electricity and didn't even have indoor plumbing. When the family needed to go to the bathroom they went to an outside shed, called an outhouse.

"We didn't have too much money back then, but we had everything else, especially love," Wilma writes in her autobiography, *Wilma*.

At the time, racism was prevalent in American society. Black people had to drink from separate water fountains and sit in the back on buses. They couldn't eat in the same restaurants as white people, and weren't considered for the same jobs as white applicants. Only one doctor in Clarksville was willing to treat black people.

When Wilma went to a grocery store, white kids sometimes taunted her.

"Hey, nigger, get out of town!"

Wilma's parents taught her and her siblings to "hold their tongue" and not respond. Sometimes, though, she and her friends fought the white bullies.

"The fights were nasty at times, very nasty," she writes.

At age six, Wilma began to notice she was very different from her friends.

"I realized that something was wrong with me," she says.

Wilma had been born prematurely, weighing four and a half pounds. Early on, she always seemed to contract serious illnesses, including scarlet fever, pneumonia, mumps, and whooping cough.

At age four, Wilma was stricken with polio, an infectious disease that today is prevented by vaccination, thanks to the work of Dr. Jonas Salk in the 1950s. At the time, though, there was no cure for polio and it severely weakened thousands of children each year, causing serious developmental problems or even death.

Wilma survived the disease, but her left leg twisted inward and she couldn't straighten it. She also lost strength in her left leg and foot. Wilma did special exercises and her devoted family gave her massages a few times a day, helping her regain strength, though most assumed she would rely on a wheelchair or leg brace her entire life.

"My doctors told me I would never walk again," Wilma later said. "My mother told me I would. I believed my mother."

With the help of her exercises and massages, Wilma did begin walking, astounding her doctors, but she was too weak to go to school. When she played with friends, sometimes they made fun of her for how different she looked.

"Some of them would start teasing me and calling me 'cripple,'" Wilma writes in her book. "But even that didn't bother [me] too often because I always had brothers and sisters around, and they would stick up for me, and the teasing would stop."

Sometimes, though, Wilma was hurt by the cruelty. At first, she cried. Eventually, the mockery gave her a new determination to succeed in life.

Someday I'll do something that will make them all take notice and put them in their places, Wilma recalled thinking.

Unable to walk for long distances, Wilma stayed home most days. Her family didn't have a television and few books were around, so there was little for her to do. Instead, Wilma spent time trying to picture a better life for herself.

"There wasn't really anything to do but dream," she writes.

When Wilma was seven, she was allowed to start second grade, though she still battled health issues. Until she was twelve, Wilma wore a steel brace on her leg, usually from the morning until she went to sleep at night. Wilma also needed to take long bus rides for treatments for her leg.

The goal was to help straighten her leg, and it was certainly working, but the brace made Wilma insecure around other young people. She also couldn't enjoy games on the playground and was forced to watch others run and play sports.

"It always reminded me that something was wrong with me," she later said, referring to the brace.

Finally, at age twelve, Wilma took the brace off for good. Until then, she had little experience with or knowledge of sports. Now Wilma was fully healthy for the first time. She went to a local playground and saw some kids playing basketball and became excited and intrigued.

"I watched them for a while, saw how much fun they were having, studied what they were doing and I said to myself, 'Wilma, tomorrow you're going to see what it feels like to play a little basketball,'" she recalled.

. . .

Wilma had spent years sitting around the house. Now that she was healthy, she threw herself into athletics, first playing on her school's basketball team and then joining the track-and-field team. Running with the team, Wilma noticed she could pass both boys and girls with ease. She even raced past her coach. It was almost like she was a superhero discovering powers she hadn't been aware of.

Wilma was the first at practice and last to leave. Sometimes, she and a boy in her school would climb a fence and sneak into a municipal stadium in the area to do even more running. Wilma was so fast she won every race she entered.

One year in high school, her team entered a meet in Alabama. Wilma was cocky and confident before the race but ended up losing in embarrassing fashion, leaving her despondent for days.

"I can't remember ever being so totally crushed," she writes.

Wilma realized she couldn't rely on natural ability. Lots of girls were fast, it turned out. She would need to outwork them and outsmart them, she decided. Wilma became even more dedicated, sometimes running twenty miles a day over local hills and farmlands. Her coach also taught her proper running techniques. Her stamina and breathing quickly improved.

Once, after winning a big meet in Philadelphia, Wilma had a chance to take a picture with Brooklyn Dodgers star Jackie Robinson, the first black baseball player in the major leagues. Robinson said he had seen Wilma race and couldn't believe she was only in high school.

"You are a fascinating runner and don't let anything or anybody keep you from running," Robinson told an overwhelmed Wilma. "I really think you have a lot of potential."

Just before her junior year in high school in 1956, when Wilma was sixteen, her coach told her something that would have been simply absurd for her to hear a few years back: She had a chance to make the US Olympic team.

Wilma had no idea what the Olympics were, or

even that nations competed against each other in various sports. The next Olympic Games were to be held that very year in Melbourne, Australia, but Wilma had never even heard of the city.

Yet Wilma had faith in her coach. If he believed she had a chance, maybe that meant she really did. The Olympic trials were in two weeks, the coach said, and Wilma agreed to go and do her best, even though he told her the competitors would be young women who were already in college with many more years of experience.

The weather was cold in Washington D.C., the site of the trials. The stadium seemed huge to Wilma, and she was intimidated by the foreign surroundings and sight of her older competitors.

But when the gun went off to signal the start of the race, Wilma ran like lightning, sprinting to a lead in the 200 meters. She did so well she made the team. Wilma was well on her way to proving to the kids in the playground who'd once mocked her that she would do something special in her life.

"From that moment on, it seemed as if I wasn't

afraid to challenge anyone, anywhere," according to Wilma.

Back home, locals were so happy for Wilma that they chipped in to buy her a suitcase, which her family didn't have, as well as some new clothes for her upcoming trip.

The team stopped in Hawaii on their way to Australia, spending a day in Honolulu. As Wilma and two African American teammates walked down the street, window-shopping, a white woman they passed looked horrified.

"What are you natives doing out in the street?" she asked, before picking up her dog and crossing the street, as if to get away from the girls. The experience left her sad the rest of the day, Wilma later said.

It wasn't the first time she had encountered racism. Some of the nicknames she had acquired, such as "The Black Gazelle" and "Mosquito," offended her.

"Racism is part of life, you deal with it," Wilma later told Jackie Joyner-Kersee, another legendary track star.

"She wouldn't let it sap her energy," Jackie says.

Her spirits high, Wilma arrived in Melbourne prepared to compete in the 200-meter race. Unfortunately, her hopes were dashed very quickly. Wilma was eliminated early on in the 200-meter trial heat, shocking and disappointing her. After her loss, she felt as though she'd let down her team, coach, and country. Wilma rooted for her teammates and vowed to come back in four years and win an individual medal.

But Wilma still had a chance to win a medal in the team relay race. When she got the baton in the race, which meant it was her turn to start running, she passed two competitors, helping her team secure a bronze medal and further fueling her determination to return to the Olympics and achieve even greater success.

Over the next few years, Wilma began college at Tennessee State, where she starred on the track team, worked on her running, and became even faster. She wasn't prepared for what would happen at the trials for the 1960 Olympic Games in Rome, Italy, however. She ran the 200 meters, plopped down next to her coach, looked up at the results, and couldn't believe her eyes:

22.9 seconds, a new world record. Wilma ended up making the US team in the 100-meter and 200-meter races, as well as the relay.

On the day before her first race in Rome, disaster struck. While stretching and jogging on a grassy field in the Italian city, Wilma stepped into a hole, turned her ankle, and heard a pop. She began crying, fearing her swollen ankle was broken.

It turned out to be a sprain. Wilma knew she had overcome much more difficult health challenges in her life. Plus, her first race was the shortest of the games, the 100 meters. She was determined to fight through the pain.

"I put it all out of my head," she says.

Tension built in the stadium before the final race. Fans weren't sure how Wilma, who was just twenty years old, would fare against top competitors from the United Kingdom, West Germany, and other nations, or if her ankle would hold up. She got off to a solid start, third in the race, and then turned it on at 50 meters, accelerating past all her rivals. Wilma ended up winning the race in eleven seconds, a world record, as the fans in Rome cheered "Vil-ma, Vil-ma," because they were not used to pronouncing the letter W.

Wilma ended up winning gold medals in all three of her Olympic events, becoming the first American woman to win that many gold medals in a single Olympic Games. Suddenly, she was an international star. She and her teammates even met Pope John XXIII in the Vatican after the games, and later she met President John F. Kennedy. Back home, the city of Clarksville hosted a parade in her honor, and over forty thousand people came to cheer on their hometown hero.

It was astounding how much had changed for Wilma in a few short years. Once, some had wondered if she would be able to walk. Now she was renowned as the fastest woman in the world.

Suddenly, Wilma was seen as a role model, especially for black and female athletes. Until Wilma's exploits, track and field was considered a sport for men only. Her remarkable story and unlikely road to success helped build nationwide interest in women's track and field and even gave a boost to the civil rights movement. After the Olympics, for example, Wilma participated in a protest in Clarksville that helped lead to full racial integration of her hometown's restaurants and public facilities. Wilma was a model of dignity and courage who impressed all Americans. Her success proved that it was pure ignorance to believe that minorities were somehow inferior to white people.

Wilma retired in 1962, at the peak of her athletic career, after beating a tough Soviet competitor at a race at Stanford University. She was the world record holder in the 100- and 200-meter events and wanted to "go out in style." A year later, she graduated from college and became an educator and coach.

While she continued to share memories of her exploits, Wilma also emphasized the importance of learning from losses and setbacks.

"Winning is great, sure, but if you are really going to do something in life, the secret is learning how to lose," Wilma once said. "If you can pick up after a crushing defeat, and go on to win again, you are going to be a champion someday."

• • •

Wilma, who passed away in 1994, continues to impact people today, inspiring stars in various sports and others in broader society. Some have read about Wilma, have watched movies featuring her exploits, or were told about her remarkable story.

Others, such as Jackie Joyner-Kersee, were lucky enough to have met Wilma. Jackie is an African American track-and-field star who overcame severe asthma and the loss of her mother as a freshman in college to become one of the US's greatest all-time athletes. Jackie says she first met Wilma during the 1984 Olympic Games when Jackie competed in the heptathlon as well as the long jump and Wilma was a television commentator. Later, Wilma took Jackie under her wing.

Jackie says Wilma paved the way for her own accomplishments, which include three Olympic gold medals, one silver medal, and two bronze medals. Like Wilma, Jackie faced racism during various parts of her career. Some even called her epithets, such as "gorilla," she says.

"I dealt with it all the time and still sometimes do," she says.

Wilma gave Jackie a model of how to deal with bigotry.

"She wasn't bitter, she rose above it. She had that grace and elegance and [was] always smiling," Jackie says. "She said it's important to take the time and breathe and not overreact [to racist comments] because there will be consequences."

Jackie says young people can take inspiration from how Wilma "had polio and still had the will and courage not just to walk, but also to run and then win three gold medals."

"She's a constant reminder that things aren't as bad as you think they are," says Jackie, who today works with inner-city elementary and middle-school kids in East St. Louis.

Wilma taught Jackie that "obstacles can become an excuse." That's true not just in athletics but also in every other aspect of life.

Wilma's lessons are as relevant today as they were back in the 1950s. Almost any kind of obstacle in life

can be overcome, no matter how imposing, with per-
sistence, dignity, and a healthy belief in one's own
abilities to succeed.

"Never underestimate the power of dreams and the
influence of the human spirit," Wilma said. "We are
all the same in this notion: The potential for greatness
lives within each of us."

RONDA ROUSEY

Ronda Rousey's first battle began with her very first breath.

Ronda was born with her umbilical cord wrapped around her neck. She was blue in the face, her air supply was cut off, and her heart stopped. Doctors rushed to help the baby, concerned she might die, as Ronda's parents watched and cried.

Little Ronda, a born fighter, managed to survive. But the doctor told her parents she suffered potential damage from the lack of oxygen reaching her brain, and Ronda might have to deal with learning disabilities later in life. At the hospital, babies are given a score of 0 to 10 to rate their health on something called an Apgar scale. Ronda's score was zero.

Ronda spent the first few years of her life unable to communicate. Her mother took her to specialists, who said being cut off from oxygen at birth might have created lasting speech difficulties. When Ronda's speech challenges continued at age three, Ronda's parents became very concerned. The sounds and words that came out of her mouth weren't what little Ronda intended.

It took a while, but her brain began to adjust. Eventually, Ronda's brain rewired itself and she began to speak like other kids.

It was the start of a childhood filled with challenges. One day that same year, Ronda's parents took her and her siblings to a hill in their neighborhood in Minot, North Dakota, to go sledding. Her father, Ron, went down first, making sure it was safe for his kids. The ride seemed smooth at first, but then, suddenly, Ron sledded over a tree trunk covered with snow, skidded to a stop at the bottom of the hill and lay flat on his back on the ground, unable to get up or even move. An ambulance came and took him to a local hospital, where doctors determined he had broken his back.

For months, Ron lay in the hospital as doctors tried

to deal with a rare disorder that made it impossible for him to stop bleeding. Even after going home, his condition deteriorated and his back gave him more problems. Ronda watched her father deal with excruciating pain and paralysis.

At age eight, Ronda's mother sat her down on the living room couch to deliver some awful and shocking news.

"Dad went to heaven," she told Ronda.

Unable to deal with the unbearable pain and with no hope in sight, Ronda's father had taken his own life. When Ronda heard the news, her legs collapsed under her and she fell to the ground.

"I cried so hard I felt like I was going to run out of tears," Ronda writes in her book, *My Fight Your Fight*.

Over the next few years, Ronda and her family did their best to recover from the tragedy.

In her period of sadness, Ronda turned to a new hobby—martial arts. Her mother, AnnMaria, had achieved athletic distinction in her youth. In 1984, at age twenty-six, AnnMaria had been the first American to win the world judo championship before giving up the sport. After her husband's death, AnnMaria married a man from California, so the family moved to Santa Monica, near Los Angeles. There, AnnMaria reconnected with old friends from her judo career and Ronda, now eleven years old, decided to follow in her mother's footsteps and try judo. Something about the sport immediately grabbed her.

At the time, Ronda was still dealing with her father's sudden death. She also was adjusting to her new home and school and was getting to know her stepfather. When Ronda played other sports, her mind wandered and she found herself thinking about her difficult life and her father's death. But judo is all about being in the moment. If your mind wanders just a bit, an opponent can pounce, throwing you to the ground in embarrassing fashion. Judo was the perfect sport for a young woman in desperate need of distraction from the upheaval of her life.

Other kids complained about the rigor of the sport, but for Ronda judo seemed almost like a vacation—a chance for her mind to focus on something other than the challenges in her life. After each grueling practice and match, Ronda couldn't wait for more. She also discovered she loved the feeling of victory. Ronda might not have been the best student, but she stood out on the judo mat with her obvious natural talent. Once, she even won a tournament by defeating each of her opponents by *ippon*, a judo term for a quick move that results in instant and dominant victory.

Her mother, AnnMaria, pushed Ronda to excel. Ronda was short and skinny, but her mother told her to ignore coaches and others who doubted her.

"You prove them wrong," AnnMaria told Ronda.

As she practiced and became stronger, kids began to bully Ronda. Some called her "Miss Man," referring to her bulging biceps and shoulders. One day, a boy crept up behind Ronda and grabbed her throat. Ronda reacted with unusual quickness and strength, throwing the boy over her hip onto the cement, stunning him.

Another time, as Ronda lugged her bassoon in the hall, an eighth-grade girl shoved and taunted her, challenging Ronda to a fight. Ronda defended herself and earned respect from her classmates for refusing to accept the abuse. Ronda dropped the eighth grader with a single punch.

Ronda continued to improve her judo skills, and at sixteen she became the youngest competitor on the US national team. She had obvious natural skills, but Ronda also had a sheer will and resilience that few could match. When Ronda broke her right hand she didn't sulk or take time away from the sport. Instead, Ronda developed an unstoppable left hook. After tearing the anterior cruciate ligament (ACL) in her knee, Ronda spent a year practicing her mat work, doing thousands of armbar moves until she had perfected them. This type of dedication would serve her well throughout her athletic career.

"Don't focus on what you can't do," Ronda says. "Focus on what you can do."

Injuries and setbacks, rather than stalling Ronda's progress, turned her into a disciplined, relentless athlete. One of her early coaches, Jimmy Pedro, notes that in judo, competitors often are pinned to the ground and have to fight to get out. Ronda battled harder than almost anyone he had ever seen.

"She had an inability to accept defeat; she hated losing more than she loved winning," he says. "Ronda just refused to accept losing. It bothered her to the point of depression."

In 2003, at age sixteen, Ronda was so focused on making the US Olympic team that she dropped out of school and traveled across the country to live with another top judo coach who resided in New Hampshire. It proved to be a very challenging period for Ronda. Alone at night, she sometimes cried and called her mother, who offered little sympathy. Uncomfortable socializing with the older players, Ronda read science fiction, drew sketches in a notebook, or watched movies on her own.

Ronda was a growing, athletic young woman with a healthy appetite. But she was wary of fighting women in her weight class, who appeared stronger than she was, so Ronda reduced her caloric intake to remain in a lower weight division.

As a result, Ronda was hungry all the time. Her coach stayed on top of her so she wouldn't gain weight. Once, when the coach, who Ronda called "Big Jim," caught Ronda eating graham crackers in the basement, he lashed out.

"You have no discipline!" Ronda recalls the coach telling her.

Racked with guilt after eating full meals, Ronda started trying to make herself vomit up her food in a bathroom toilet. At first it didn't work. But Ronda persisted and the purging became a habit. After a period of constant hunger, Ronda would eat a meal, and then just as she began to feel full, she would force her entire meal out of her stomach, an incredibly dangerous routine that threatened Ronda's long-term health. This very serious eating disorder is known as bulimia.

Ronda's judo skills were improving, despite her developing bulimic condition. By 2004 she had climbed to the top of the national rankings and earned a spot on the US Olympic team, becoming the youngest competitor in the entire Athens Olympic field. Still trying to keep her weight down, Ronda was starving and thirsty as the games began. At one point, she was so dehydrated that her body couldn't even manage to sweat.

Ronda finished ninth in the Olympics, an impressive feat for someone so young, especially considering she was barely eating or drinking at the time. But Ronda, striving for greatness, left Athens dejected. She had expected to win a medal and couldn't shake her disappointment.

"I had lost tournaments before, but I had never felt this level of crushing devastation," Ronda says.

Following the Olympics, Ronda's frustration lingered. She frequently fought with her mother and eventually ran away from home. She stayed with a friend's family but eventually was kicked out, moving from place to place while lugging two duffel bags carrying all her belongings. Lonely and struggling to make her weight level, Ronda turned to a new boyfriend for support. For a while, he gave her comfort. Over time, however, the boyfriend turned emotionally abusive, preying on Ronda's weaknesses, perhaps because he was jealous of her judo success.

"Boy, you're getting fat," he would tease.

In some ways, the turmoil spurred Ronda in her career.

Ronda had a "chip on her shoulder," Jimmy Pedro, her early coach, says. "She was out to prove something. She's good at being the underdog."

Only when Ronda competed did she feel in control and at ease. The fights also gave her an outlet for her mounting frustrations. In April 2006, Ronda won the World Cup tournament in Birmingham, England, her greatest achievement in a year full of triumphs. But as soon as the thrill of a victory faded, Ronda immediately began worrying about how she was going to make her weight level in the next competition. Ronda started wearing plastic sweats and blasting hot water in her bathtub to increase her sweat production. She'd often go two days without food, only drinking black coffee, trying to shed pounds. Other times she would eat and then purge her meal.

All the while, no one in her life warned her to improve her unhealthy lifestyle.

At a tournament in Vienna something surprising happened. Ronda missed the regular weigh-in and was forced to compete at a weight class fifteen pounds above her usual level. Ronda was nervous to go up against bigger fighters, but at least she could eat a full breakfast before fighting. The nourishment seemed to work—Ronda won the entire tournament and turned in one of her best performances ever.

Ronda realized she had unnecessarily weakened herself, potentially causing serious damage to her health, to fight at a lower weight level. It turned out she could handle the larger competitors. Even more important, Ronda was having fun for the first time in a while. Good health translated into good feelings. And the happier she was, the better she performed, a crucial life lesson.

"For the first time in as long as I could remember, I was enjoying myself," Ronda says. "My focus was just on competing and having fun."

Ronda stormed into Beijing for the 2008 Olympics and came away with both a bronze medal and a feeling of accomplishment.

After returning home, Ronda picked up odd jobs and tried to figure out her future. She was working in a bar one night, watching ESPN's *SportsCenter*, when highlights from a mixed martial arts match aired. MMA, a full-contact combat sport that allows punching, kicking, kneeing, and elbowing, borrows from other sports, including judo. At the time, MMA was growing in popularity and Ronda became intrigued.

She asked one of her judo coaches to help her train to compete as an MMA fighter. "You're wasting your talent," he told her. "This plan of yours is never going to work."

Ronda's mother was even less encouraging.

"It's the stupidest . . . idea I've ever heard in my entire life," she said, noting that there were no female fighters in the Ultimate Fighting Championship (UFC), which promoted the most popular MMA events.

Ronda had valuable judo skills but needed to learn many others, including striking, or hitting, opponents. In MMA, fighters use their hands, elbows, legs, and feet to deliver powerful blows. Ronda eventually convinced a coach to work with her, and she focused on her new sport. She had a new goal: to be a star MMA fighter. Juggling three jobs, Ronda pushed herself like never before.

In her first amateur fight in 2010, Ronda approached her opponent in the middle of the ring, or, as they call it in MMA, the cage. Ronda fended off a kick, grabbed her opponent's leg, and threw the woman to the ground. Ronda pounced and her opponent tried to get away. In pain, she tapped on the mat, signaling that she was giving up. Ronda had won in just 23 seconds. She felt overwhelming happiness.

Ronda kept on winning, turning pro five months later. She was quick and talented, but so were many of her competitors. The qualities that separated Ronda from the pack were her drive and willingness to work harder than others. When she was preparing for a match, Ronda endured grueling six-hour training sessions, six days a week. To hone her boxing skills, she hit the heavy bag and did "mitt work," punching a sparring partner's boxing mitts, to hone her reflexes and technique. Ronda also worked on her footwork, sparred with opponents, and worked on various other boxing skills. She stretched, jumped rope, and did two thousand crunches a day to strengthen her abs.

Soon, Ronda was fighting tougher competition

as part of Strikeforce, a top MMA organization. Her first fight, against Sarah D'Alelio, was at the Las Vegas Palms hotel in front of thousands of fans. Ronda quickly locked an armbar—a powerful move in which Ronda placed her legs across D'Alelio's chest, grabbed her arm, and locked it up, pressuring her elbow joint while inflicting intense pain. Ronda was awarded a technical knockout after 25 seconds but it wasn't clear if D'Alelio had "tapped out," or given up.

The decision by the judge caused fans to boo lustily. Ronda resolved to be even more ferocious in future battles, to ensure there were no doubts about who had emerged victorious.

"I was so . . . pissed that I did a cool flying armbar and [the match] was tarnished," Ronda says. "I was like, that's it. I'm not gonna be nice ever."

On March 3, 2012, Ronda took on Miesha Tate, the world champion, in Columbus, Ohio, with 431,000 fans tuned in on Showtime to watch. Tate came out swinging, showing little fear and landing several painful blows. Ronda withstood the barrage and managed to get her arm around Tate's neck, throwing her to the ground and pouncing. Ronda used her powerful thighs to hold Tate down for a while, but Tate recovered, standing over Ronda while landing more blows and weakening Ronda, who was used to quick victories and had never fought so long or endured so much pain in the cage.

But Ronda managed to outlast Tate, winning on another armbar submission to capture the championship. Scanning the crowd, Ronda found her mother, standing and beaming with happiness. Just as fans around the country had embraced Ronda's growing prominence in her new sport, so too had her mother.

"The worst moments of my life brought me to the best times," Ronda says. "Loss. Heartbreak. Injury. I had come to understand every event was necessary to guide me to where I am today."

Ronda was gaining recognition and even appeared on the cover of *ESPN The Magazine*'s annual body issue. But the most popular MMA organization, Ultimate Fighting Championship, still wouldn't consider featuring female fighters. When UFC president Dana White was asked if he ever would allow women to fight, he laughed and said, "Never."

That year, Ronda approached White at an event. Ronda spent 45 minutes trying to convince him to create a women's division. She was passionate, charismatic, and ambitious, describing how she could lead the way and help the women's division gain a following.

Fifteen minutes into the conversation, White says he was convinced. He could tell that twenty-five-year-old Ronda was likable and a potential fan favorite. She had the talent and a determination to be a champion. Put all of that together and she had the makings of a future global star.

"If we're ever going to do it, this is the woman to do so," White later recalled in an interview with ESPN.

Ronda's first UFC fight in February 2013 was a championship bout against Liz Carmouche in UFC's eight-sided enclosure, which it called "the Octagon." Ronda knew it would be difficult. Carmouche was a tough, twenty-eight-year-old US Marine who served three tours of duty in the Middle East, including in war-torn Iraq. Heading into the match, she had an 8–2 career record.

Less than a minute into the fight, Ronda was on the defensive. Carmouche jumped on Ronda's back and she found herself losing balance as Carmouche yanked her neck straight up. Ronda's sinuses popped and her teeth cut into her upper lip. She could feel her jaw dislocating.

"I was literally on the verge of having my neck snapped in half," Ronda recalls.

The screaming crowd waited for Ronda to give up. She refused.

Ronda somehow pushed Carmouche off her back, backflipped to avoid a leg lock, and put Carmouche in a side headlock. Then she delivered a series of painful punches, scoring repeated blows to Carmouche's head, before her opponent tapped out.

In her very first UFC match, Ronda Rousey had shown the world that she was a force to be reckoned with and wouldn't go down easily.

In a highly anticipated 2013 rematch with Tate in Las Vegas's MGM Grand Garden Arena, Ronda landed a flurry of punches, winning the fight in a three-round epic battle that is considered key in cementing the place of women in mixed martial arts.

By 2015 Ronda was 12–0 and was one of the highest-paid athletes in the sports world. One fight lasted 16 seconds, another just 14. Ronda was UFC's top financial draw, headlining matches above top male fighters. The *Wall Street Journal* said she could be considered "one of the most important athletes on the planet" and "a gender pioneer in her sport."

Ronda hosted *Saturday Night Live*, was featured in *Sports Illustrated*'s swimsuit issue, appeared in major motion pictures, and modeled for Buffalo jeans. That year, Ronda was the third-most Googled person.

She had no hint of the dramatic challenges still ahead.

In November 2015, Ronda squared off against Holly Holm in Melbourne, Australia. Ronda was heavily favored going into the match—no one thought Holm had a chance of stealing a win. But in the second round of the highest-attended event in UFC history, Holm, an ex-boxer, stunned Ronda with a devastating high kick to the neck that knocked Ronda out in stunning fashion. She lost the match as well as her undefeated record in a fight the *New York Times* called "an epic shock."

Ronda was 12–1 in her career and remained a worldwide superstar, but inside, she was a mess. It had been a long time since Ronda had suffered a serious setback, and the loss sent her spiraling emotionally. She was so depressed that she went into seclusion, questioned her worth, and even considered suicide, she later told talk show host Ellen DeGeneres.

"What am I anymore?" Ronda asked herself, she tearfully recalled on the show.

Slowly, Ronda set her sights on a comeback. Focused and in the best shape of her life, she took on Amanda Nunes, a Brazilian jiujitsu black belt who had beaten Holm to become the new champion. Four thousand fans came to the prefight weigh-in day, most cheering for Ronda and booing Nunes, who wore a lion's mask while stepping on the scales, an apparent effort to intimidate Ronda.

On a Saturday night at T-Mobile Arena in Las Vegas in late December 2016, thirteen months after Ronda's loss to Holm, Ronda's comeback quest began.

It wasn't meant to be, though. Early on, Nunes pounced on Ronda with a series of jabs to her face that sent her stumbling in the cage. Ronda's reflexes were off. She didn't move her head quickly enough, doing a poor job of defending herself. Nunes pounded Ronda, landing one vicious punch after another with her powerful right hand, an outright pummeling.

Ronda was knocked down and couldn't get up, shocking the crowd. It took 48 seconds for the referee to stop the match and award Nunes the victory. Around the arena, men and women began to cry, sensing the end of an era.

As Ronda leaned on the cage after the fight, bracing herself, Nunes raced over and grabbed her by the shoulders. She was thanking Ronda, not hurting her.

"You did so much for this sport," Nunes said.

White, the UFC chief, also embraced Ronda, despite the blood and sweat that covered much of her body.

"I love you so much and whatever you want to do

next, I got your back," he recalls telling Ronda. "You built this. This doesn't exist without you. You're the best decision I ever made."

After Ronda's loss, fans, commentators, and others discovered a new appreciation for all Ronda had accomplished. At one point, the UFC didn't even want women to battle. But Ronda was a trailblazer, paving the way for others to follow in her footsteps and gain their own fame and fortune from mixed martial arts. She made it acceptable for women to fight in the sport, just like men. She even made it cool, something for a new generation of young girls to aspire to. Strong women now were respected, not harassed. Ronda's legacy was secure.

"Rousey can hold her head high for what she has meant to women's MMA," the *New York Post* wrote the next day. "Nunes, in many ways, is a product of Rousey's impact on MMA . . . Because of Rousey, women have become a top attraction."

Sometimes in life, loss can bring as much respect and appreciation as victory.

• • •

After the brutal loss, Ronda avoided the media and stayed out of the limelight, raising worries among her fans. Her new home in Venice Beach, California, was vandalized with indecipherable black graffiti, adding to her misery. It was clear Ronda was dealing with her most imposing setback yet.

But signs emerged that Ronda was preparing for life's next challenges. She turned thirty and spoke of wanting to get married, have children, and start a new life. Movie roles were waiting for her, along with other projects. Ronda had made tens of millions of dollars from her victories, endorsements, and other projects and was a role model, demonstrating the strength and perseverance of all women. Dana White spoke with her and said she was content and in good spirits.

Ronda released a statement to ESPN indicating she was coming to grips with her shattering loss. She also shared lessons about how to deal with disappointment.

"Returning to not just fighting, but winning, was my entire focus this past year," she wrote. "However, sometimes—even when you prepare and give everything you have and want something so badly—it doesn't work how you planned. I take pride in seeing how far the women's division has come in the UFC and commend all the women who have been part of making this possible, including Amanda. I need to take some time to reflect and think about the future. Thank you for believing in me and understanding."

Around that time, Ronda sent a quote to her fans on Instagram from an address J. K. Rowling, author of the Harry Potter series, gave in 2008 at a Harvard University commencement speech:

"I was set free, because my greatest fear had already been realized, and I was still alive . . . And so rock bottom became the solid foundation on which I rebuilt my life."

Ronda's message: She had suffered a devastating loss and hit rock bottom. But she was alive and kicking and wasn't going to give up. Just as Rowling found that failure in her own pursuits enabled her to focus on her true love, writing, Ronda was suggesting that her life still held opportunity and potential. Giving up wasn't an option. She was going to rebuild and find new success. If it wasn't in the Octagon, it would be somewhere else.

Awards, accolades, and victories are obvious measures of success. But another kind of triumph is the ability to deal with and learn from abject failure. In some ways, Ronda Rousey's greatest strength, even more than her fighting abilities, was her refusal to stay down even after she'd fallen.

SWIN CASH

As she stepped onto the basketball court, Swin Cash could hear the whispers.

She felt out of place. Her sneakers were beaten up and her outfit was a hand-me-down. She could feel other players staring and talking about her.

Swin knew what they were saying.

Born in McKeesport, Pennsylvania, a suburb of Pittsburgh, Swin was raised by her mother, Cynthia, who was just a seventeen-year-old high school student when she gave birth to her first child. She named her Swintayla, or "astounding woman" in Swahili, a language used in parts of the family's native Africa.

At the time, Cynthia was a high school basketball player, a left-handed star dreaming of scoring a scholarship to play ball in college. Determined to keep her life on track, Cynthia returned to the court just two months after giving birth, to the amazement of her coach and teammates. Living at home with her parents, Cynthia placed Swin's crib next to her own bed, leaning on her family for support.

With great focus, Cynthia managed to keep up with her classes, work hard to support her baby, attend to her studies, and play basketball. Even with all of these responsibilities, Cynthia graduated from high school.

Cynthia longed to go to college, but Swin's father wasn't around to help, and as a single mother, she felt pressure to find a job to help support her young daughter. Cynthia reluctantly enrolled in a trade school and took courses at a local community college, hoping to learn about computers. But she had trouble finding a job and her anxiety built.

Eventually, Cynthia found a maintenance job at a senior living center operated by the McKeesport

Housing Authority. She had given up her dream of college and basketball but was thankful to land the job and felt she was teaching Swin a lesson in how to be a responsible parent. Each day, Cynthia pulled on a pair of work pants and an orange Housing Authority T-shirt and left for work. On hot summer days, she pulled a black spandex cap over her head to hold in the sweat.

Cynthia and Swin moved to the Harrison Village projects, a neighborhood that frequently witnessed violence. The region had seen a surge in unemployment after the local steelmaking industry suffered, sparking a flight from the area. Some girls in Swin's school carried knives, while others kept rocks in their socks, to intimidate classmates. Swin's mother encouraged her to focus on building a better life for herself, hoping school, sports, and church would keep Swin out of trouble. "Give your maximum effort and try to avoid the mistakes I made," her mother stressed.

On the basketball court in grade school, Swin modeled her game after her mother's. Swin was a righty but she dribbled with her left hand as much as possible, mimicking her mother. Swin also adopted her mother's fearless style, crashing the boards with abandon and posting up aggressively. After school and on weekends, the mother and daughter went at it in ferocious games of one-on-one, neither giving an inch.

Cynthia almost always won, but by seventh grade it was clear Swin was developing into a formidable talent with a game honed by spirited games against eight male cousins. When Swin joined a basketball team at the local recreation center, she couldn't help standing out—she was the only girl in the entire league.

"I was not [just] the only female, but I also was an African American from a humble upbringing," she says.

Swin and her friends didn't have much money and often couldn't find an open basketball court, so they adjusted. Sometimes Swin cut the bottom of a milk carton and affixed it to the top of a garbage can to act as a makeshift backboard.

Before her freshman year of high school, Swin joined an Amateur Athletic Union (AAU) summer league to test her game against the best players in the region. On the first day of practice, Swin realized it was going to be hard for her to fit in. Her clothes and sneakers were older and less impressive than those of her teammates. Swin could sense the other players staring or whispering. She knew what they were saying.

"Kids could figure out how much my outfit cost," Swin says. "A lot of the kids had the best shoes and clothes . . . People had pity for me, I was a kid from the projects."

When she could, Swin's mother came to games and rooted hard from the sidelines. "Come on, Skee!" she screamed, using Swin's nickname.

Other times, though, Swin's mother missed games for work. Parents and teammates couldn't understand how Cynthia could miss her daughter's big games, especially since Swin had emerged as the team's star. Swin knew they were talking about her and her mother behind their backs. Parents sometimes approached Swin to ask if she wanted to go out to eat with them after a game. They meant well, but Swin wasn't sad.

"I looked around and knew people felt sorry for me," she says. "I could see how hard my mother was working to make a better life for me . . . I was confident in who I was, even if people felt sorry for me."

Swin had a loving family, clothing on her back, and enough food on the table. Others may have felt bad for her, but Swin felt comfortable about herself.

"I didn't have a lot of things growing up, but I never felt I had less. I was just growing up a different way," Swin says. "My mom was doing the best she could, I was okay not having the Air Jordans that came out last week, I never felt insecure."

Swin's mother emphasized how basketball might be Swin's ticket to a better life—as long as Swin didn't make mistakes off the court like she had. Cynthia never managed to get the basketball scholarship she had dreamed of, but through practice and discipline, maybe Swin could.

"It was all about setting goals in life," Cynthia told the *Hartford Courant*. "In Swin's case, it was a college scholarship."

In high school, Swin's coach at McKeesport Area

High School, Gerald Grayson, quickly recognized Swin's developing talent. Coach Grayson emphasized a defense-first approach, and his players were relentless.

"Don't let anyone outwork you!" Coach Grayson often bellowed at his players.

Swin's teammates appreciated her work ethic, a grit and determination passed down by her mother, and defenders began to fear her. Searching for a way to stop her, rivals began overplaying her right-hand drive. Swin responded by going hard to her left, the heated games against her mother paying off.

By her sophomore year, Swin was on her way to a towering height of six foot one, and buzz about her potential reached nearby Pittsburgh and beyond. One day before her junior year of high school, as Swin played a pickup game with her AAU summer teammates, she noticed a short, older man in the gym watching the game carefully. Later, Swin found out it was Geno Auriemma, the famed coach of the University of Connecticut's basketball team. He was there to see if Swin might be good enough to play for his team, the perennial champions of women's college basketball.

Swin couldn't believe Coach Auriemma was there to scout her. "I began to realize that I was going to have an opportunity to do something special with basketball," she says.

After graduation, Swin enrolled at Connecticut and helped lead the Huskies to national championships in 2000 and 2002. In 2002, Swin was voted an All-American and the Most Outstanding Player in the Final Four, posting 20 points and thirteen rebounds in the national championship game, an 82–70 win over Oklahoma that completed Connecticut's undefeated 39–0 season.

When she graduated in 2002, Swin ended her college career as the storied Huskies program's seventh all-time leading scorer with 1,583 points. After graduation, she was selected by the Detroit Shock with the number two overall pick in the 2002 WNBA draft. Swin had achieved the goal her mother had set out for her. Walking onto the draft-day stage, she could see that the woman who'd always believed in her was filled with pride.

But Swin's professional career got off to a rocky

start. Her team, the Detroit Shock, began the 2002 season on a thirteen-game losing streak. Within a matter of two weeks, morale sank and management scrambled for solutions. The team switched coaches, hiring former NBA center Bill Laimbeer, who almost immediately named Swin the team's captain, making it clear the Shock would rebuild around Swin.

The move stunned her teammates, fans, and the media. Yes, Swin had won two national titles, but she was still a *rookie*, they kept saying. Rookies are expected to earn the respect of peers and rivals in the pro game; they're not asked to lead veteran teammates just *ten* games into their debut season.

It's hard enough adjusting to the pro game—it's even more difficult when teammates grumble about you in the locker room. Some of Swin's teammates even began to isolate Swin, refusing to speak to her. Sometimes they went out for dinner by themselves, leaving Swin to fend for herself.

"There was real resentment," Swin says. "It was a very difficult situation."

Swin tried to ignore the criticism and work even

harder on her game, setting a new goal for herself: prove to her teammates that she deserved to be the team's captain.

"I just kept plugging away," Swin says. "I came from a college program that drilled into me the need to be selfless." It had also taught her to not worry about criticism.

Swin even sympathized with her teammates, despite their harsh treatment of her. After all, there was so much attention and excitement surrounding her, but Swin's career had barely even begun.

"I was getting crowned as the 'next thing' without proving anything yet," she says.

It turned out that Swin Cash would meet the hype and then some.

Just a year later, the Shock won twenty-five games and lost nine, winning their first WNBA title. Swin and her teammates upset the defending champion, the Los Angeles Sparks, in a final game that drew the largest crowd in WNBA history. She led the team in scoring and made the All-Star game, cementing her position as one of the league's top players. Just as important, her team finally embraced her, accepting Swin as their true captain.

Over the next three years, Swin made the US Olympic basketball team and helped lead the squad to a gold medal in Athens, Greece.

Swin seemed on top of the world. She traveled home to McKeesport as the city rededicated Harrison Village's recreation center in her name, painting Olympic rings on the building's front.

Swin had no idea how quickly things would change.

Disaster struck a few weeks before the 2004 playoffs when Swin fell during a game, tearing her anterior cruciate ligament (ACL), one of the knee's four main ligaments. Just when it felt like she was on top of the world, Swin had taken a huge fall both literally and figuratively.

Without Swin—who had posted a career-high field goal percentage of 46.9 percent that year and close to 17 points a game—Detroit was eliminated in the first round against the New York Liberty.

After surgery, Swin lost both weight and muscle. She dedicated herself to rehabilitating her knee, but the effects of the injury lasted longer than she expected. Swin scored under 6 points per game in the 2005 season and just 10.5 points per game in 2006, though the Shock did win the championship that year. By 2007, Swin had developed back pain due to the impact of the injury. She barely told anyone about the herniated disc in her back, afraid fans and the media would think she was giving an excuse for her poor play. Swin still remembered when she'd been on the receiving end of whispered insults all those years back at her first AAU summer league practice. She thought it best to keep her head down and push through the injury.

"At the time, all I remember was the pain," Swin recalls. "I wasn't playing my best . . . I felt isolated and alone. My body wasn't the same. My game wasn't the same."

Swin's relationship with Coach Laimbeer quickly deteriorated. He was a demanding coach who wanted more from Swin. She managed to boost her scoring to a respectable 11.1 points per game that season, with over six rebounds a game, but it wasn't nearly Swin's best. Her coach let her know it on a regular basis.

"Imagine playing a basketball game with a hundred-pound jacket on your back and a myriad of thoughts running through your mind," Swin wrote in her book, *Humble Journey*. "It hurt to sit, to walk, and to run, basically to do anything."

Looking for an explanation for the pain, Swin had an MRI procedure that allowed doctors to view the body in finer detail. The doctor called with the results—and Swin wasn't prepared for what she was about to hear.

"I saw something on your kidney," the doctor said. "It's a tumor. You have to come in immediately so we can determine if it's cancerous."

Suddenly, Swin couldn't hear a thing. Her entire world went silent. She was so stunned—so scared—that the doctor asked if she was still on the phone. In that moment, all Swin could think about was her aunt who had died of cancer. Now Swin worried the disease might claim her, as well.

After a series of tests, doctors determined that

Swin's tumor was malignant. If the cancer wasn't removed, it could spread through her body and her life would be at risk, they said. But there was good news—doctors said they were confident they could remove the cancer. In fact, she was lucky—if it hadn't been for the back pain, the cancer might have continued to grow and spread, doctors told her.

Swin rejoined her team, prepared to remove the tumor after the season. She was determined to keep her diagnosis a secret, telling only Coach Laimbeer and Detroit's team trainer.

"I wasn't comfortable talking about it; I was going through a difficult time," Swin says. "I was nervous and trying to process it myself, and I didn't want anyone to feel sorry for me."

Despite her health issues, Coach Laimbeer didn't treat her any differently—he continued to ride her and tell Swin how disappointed he was in her performance. She tried to stay positive and trust that she would fully recover after the cancer was removed, as her doctors promised. But sometimes Swin couldn't fully concentrate. In the second game of the Eastern

Conference Finals, Coach Laimbeer benched Swin, claiming she wasn't playing hard enough, a final insult in an awful year. In front of twenty-thousand fans in Detroit, Swin and her teammates were blown out by 19 points, ousted from the playoffs on their home court.

Two days after the season ended, still feeling the sting of that painful loss, a terrified Swin drove to the hospital for surgery to remove the tumor on her kidney.

Thankfully, the operation went well, but Swin knew she had to focus on recovering from surgery, once again, and also would have to deal with her continued back pain. She also concluded that her relationship with Coach Laimbeer couldn't be salvaged. She had felt hurt when he'd benched her and questioned her hustle, even though he knew about all the pain and problems Swin was dealing with.

Detroit was a perennial championship contender, but if the locker room continued to be a dark place for Swin, she decided it would be too hard for her to stay with the team while dealing with her continued health challenges.

"I'd rather have peace of mind and happiness more than another [championship] ring," Swin says. "I realized that my health would not improve if my professional life did not change."

Swin requested a trade, and in early 2008 she was sent to the Seattle Storm for the draft rights to the number four pick in the 2008 WNBA draft. Swin was certain she could help her new team and prove she was worthy of making the US roster for the 2008 Olympics that summer.

Severe back pain persisted, though, affecting her play.

"Sharp movements would feel like someone was stabbing me with a steak knife," she says.

Swin turned to painkillers and injections, hoping to avoid surgery that would eliminate her from consideration for the Olympic team. But she started losing muscle mass. Pain led to stress. Stress led to more weight loss.

"Weight loss just caused more pain, mentally and physically," Swin says.

One day that season, she received a phone call she wasn't expecting.

"I'm calling to inform you that the committee has made their decisions about the US Olympic team," Carol Callan, head of the women's national team, said, Swin recalls. "Unfortunately, you weren't chosen as one of our twelve players."

Swin was crushed. She wasn't even chosen as an alternate to replace a player in case of injury.

"I felt like I had swallowed a bomb that exploded," Swin recalls. "I couldn't speak."

For days, Swin sat in her apartment crying. She was angry and in pain and felt very much alone. Swin was twenty-eight years old and for the first time in her life felt like an utter failure. It was the lowest point in her life, she says.

"There were a lot of times when my face was planted on the floor in tears," Swin told the *New York Times*. "You cry out to God and you're trying to understand, 'Why is this happening to me?'"

Slowly, Swin began dealing with her difficulties, trying to get past them.

"It was a lot of prayer, a lot of family, and a reevaluation of my life," she says.

Swin's Olympic dream had been crushed, but sometimes from disappointment comes opportunity. Swin was asked to be a television analyst for NBC for the Olympic Games. It gave Swin valuable experience for a future career in broadcasting and allowed her to take a step back from the daily game.

She gained perspective and became more "grounded," she says.

"I learned that things aren't always as bad as they seem, and they're also not as good," she says.

At an event in New York, Swin met Teresa Edwards, a former star basketball player who was a member of the US Olympic Committee. Swin opened up about her frustrations, and Edwards offered encouragement, promising to work with Swin to help her recapture her former level of play.

"Hearing myself talk it out with Tee was just the form of therapy that I needed," Swin says.

Swin decided to change her perspective. Yes, she had gone through a tough time and was still dealing with challenges, but she wasn't going to feel sorry for herself. She'd set new goals, just as her mother had taught her, and work to reach them by working even harder on and off the court.

"I had a revelation," Swin says. "I wouldn't be a victim any longer . . . I had to look within myself and make things happen."

Her biggest goal: make the 2012 Olympic team and prove the skeptics wrong.

"I had a chip on my shoulder that I used for motivation," Swin says. "The naysayers drove me."

Swin found happiness returning to McKeesport, a city that was facing economic challenges. She established a charity, Cash for Kids, that empowers children to lead healthier lifestyles and become leaders in their communities. The charity sponsors activities in health and fitness, provides mentors, and uses sports to motivate and educate children. Sometimes young people traveled to visit Swin. They joined her at museums and other cultural institutions and then watched her play.

Before the 2009 season, Swin finally had surgery to repair her ailing back, embracing a grueling routine in subsequent months to rehabilitate her body. A year later, the Seattle Storm enjoyed one of the most dominant seasons in WNBA history, posting a league-best 28–6 record as Swin scored nearly fourteen points a game along with six rebounds to cap off one of her best years in the league.

In the playoffs, Seattle went on a 7–0 run, sweeping Atlanta for the title, with Swin making critical plays in many games, more proof to the doubters of how well she could play when healthy.

After the game, as fans cheered wildly and teammates embraced, Swin took a moment to remember the lowest moment of her life, just two years earlier, when she'd cried on her couch, alone and despondent, after being told she had been left off the 2008 Olympic team.

"It all flashed in that moment and felt so good," Swin says.

Swin continued to return to Western Pennsylvania to attend camps and leagues run by her nonprofit, announcing games on a loudspeaker and cheering for the kids. Swin gave children her e-mail address, allowed them to be her Facebook friend, and forged bonds with girls and boys going through their own tough times.

In 2012, on a visit to her hometown, Swin heard her cell phone ring—it was a call from a representative of the US Olympic basketball team.

Swin broke down, tears of joy falling down her face. She had made the women's basketball squad for that year's Olympics, becoming the second-oldest member of the team. But the celebration was only beginning— that summer, Swin and her teammates brought home the gold once again.

It was a lesson, Swin says, in how life's lowest moments can make us stronger.

"I wouldn't change anything that's happened to me," she told the *New York Times*. "Whenever it's raining, when it stops, you get to the other side, and you see this rainbow, and you see this sunshine, and then that's when you're just smiling."

In June 2016, after four more years of play in the WNBA, Swin, the winner of two titles in Detroit, one in Seattle and two Olympic gold medals, was named by the league as one of the twenty greatest players in its history.

When she announced her retirement that year, the *New York Times* said, "few players have matched [her] influence and accomplishments."

Swin says young people have their own unique challenges they need to deal with, some of which rival those she overcame.

"Today, kids have so much pressure from their peers."

She urges children and teens "to seek out knowledge and wisdom from people older and even peers . . . young people expect to have it all together but it's important to put time into education and sports, to become a better person *and* athlete."

Be kind to each other. The girl next to you is likely going through the same things you are, Swin says.

"Women are being rated by society all the time," Swin says. "We need to pay less attention to that and have more compassion [for] each other."

Most of all, Swin emphasizes that even those who come from "humble beginnings," can find success, just as she did.

Yet Swin says there's something that brings her more joy than her medals and victories ever could. "It's how I can share the victories with my mother," she says. "Every time I see her, I can see her pride."

In 2015, when Swin married her longtime boyfriend and the band played the traditional father-daughter dance at her wedding, Swin brought her mother onto the floor. They danced to Celine Dion's "Because You Loved Me."

On that day, Swin's heart was full. All of the sacrifices her mother had made, all of the hard work and dedication, paved a road to success for Swin.

KERRI STRUG

The US team's shot at winning the Olympic gold medal wasn't supposed to come down to Kerri Strug. She knew it, her coaches knew it, and all the fans in the Olympic stadium knew it.

Dominique Moceanu was the prodigy of the American gymnastics team. Shannon Miller and Dominique Dawes were the acknowledged emerging stars, commanding most of the attention and accolades.

Then there was Kerri, the quiet and sometimes overlooked member of the 1996 women's Olympic team. Sure, in 1992, at age fourteen, Kerri had been a solid contributor and the youngest member of a 1992 Olympic squad that won a bronze medal at the Barcelona Olympics. In fact, Kerri had been one of the top female gymnasts in the country for several years and a member of the American gymnastics team from 1991 to 1995.

But some experts questioned her abilities, potential, and dedication. A four-foot-nine gymnast from Tucson, Arizona, Kerri didn't seem to have the fearlessness or threshold for pain of some of her teammates. She spent a few years in high school living at home without a dedicated coach. She also didn't seem to have the same level of talent as the other girls. The American team was nicknamed "the Magnificent Seven," but everyone knew Kerri wasn't the team's most important gymnast.

"Mentally, I wasn't as tough as other competitors," Kerri acknowledges. "I was always great in training but my competitions weren't as good."

A US women's gymnastics team had never won an Olympic team gold medal, but 1996 was the year they had been waiting for. The nation had spent four years counting down to these games, when the American women finally would outlast fierce rivals, including Russia. At one point in the team competition, the US lead seemed so insurmountable that some Russian gymnasts, who had dominated the sport for years, were close to tears.

Then everything changed. Moceanu fell twice, stunning fans. A comfortable US lead quickly evaporated. Suddenly, the US team's chances of winning gold rested solely on Kerri's shoulders as she began the vault exercise. Most of the thirty-two thousand in the crowd were on their feet as Kerri took a deep breath and sprinted down a seventy-five-foot runway. She launched herself into a challenging vault, carrying the hopes of the nation along with her.

The fans had no idea they were about to see one of the greatest and most dramatic moments in Olympics history.

From age three, Kerri had participated in gymnastics, enrolling in a Mom and Tot's class, following in the footsteps of her older sister, Lisa.

By eight, Kerri was working with a local coach and winning competitions.

"Until twelve, I just loved it," Kerri says.

It seemed clear that Kerri had a shot at the Olympics if she kept improving, though there were trade-offs in her decision to focus on the sport.

"It was a big sacrifice," Kerri says. "I didn't have a normal social life and I had a strict diet."

In January 1991, at age thirteen, Kerri joined the US national team and moved to Houston to train with legendary coach Bela Karolyi.

"If you're going to leave home, you might as well come to the best [coach]," Kerri says, explaining the move.

The youngest of three children, Kerri was close to her parents, and it was difficult to be hundreds of miles away from them. Kerri, who lived with host families while training in Houston, says she never felt so alone. Many nights, she called her family crying, saying she wanted to come home. Kerri's parents said she could return any time she wanted, hoping to relax her. She decided to try to get through the experience one day at a time.

"Let me wait a bit and see," Kerri told her parents, hoping the situation would get better.

Kerri's mother flew out to Houston to comfort her daughter, but the trip was long and she couldn't visit frequently.

At one point, the relationship between Kerri and gymnastics was pure love. Now, with Kerri deeply homesick and frustrated, it was "love-hate," she says.

Is it all worth it? Kerri wondered some days.

Kerri knew that the career of a female gymnast generally is short and most peak in their teenage years, so if she decided to continue training, she would need to go all out to have a chance at making the Olympic team. After doing some soul-searching, she decided to stick with the sport she'd loved for most of her life.

"If I was going to make the sacrifice I wanted to do it 100 percent," she says. "I didn't want to look back and say, if only I had trained harder and with the very best I would have done better, so I gave it my full commitment."

Kerri worked out as many as seven days a week, eight hours a day. Coach Bela and his wife, Martha, scrutinized everything Kerri and her teammates ate and even dictated when they went to sleep each night.

They had little free time. Munching on frozen strawberries or staying up late on Saturday night to watch the comedy show *Saturday Night Live* was one of the few indulgences Kerri was allowed. She rarely ate pizza, but when she did on a special occasion, she had to pick the cheese off the slice.

Over time, Kerri says she developed "eating issues."

"I was muscular and back then everyone looked like ballet dancers, with clean lines; my coach was into thin and graceful and tiny," Kerri says. "I was eating good food but you get desperate and you begin eliminating caloric intake and doing more cardio."

Beyond the challenge of following a strict diet, Kerri also had to withstand constant, and often harsh, criticism. Sometimes Coach Bela screamed at Kerri, especially if she performed poorly in a competition or had a bad workout.

"You know he's just trying to motivate you, but months and weeks of hearing it is hard," she says. "The coaches didn't coddle me. I was in a lot of pain all the time and I used to ask why he's making me do fifteen vaults, not just ten."

Having already decided to keep training, Kerri continued to improve and her chances of making the 1992 Barcelona Olympics seemed good. But on the final rotation on the last day of the Olympic trials in Baltimore in June of that year, Kerri fell while competing in one of her strongest events, the floor exercise, putting her Olympics participation in jeopardy. Kerri managed to make the team, though she didn't participate in individual competitions, and earned a team bronze medal. All in all, it was a bittersweet competition—though she'd won a team medal, she hadn't had a chance to show off her true potential as an individual.

That year, Coach Bela retired and Kerri considered giving up the sport. She didn't think she'd be able to make the 1996 Olympics and looked forward to a new life with different hobbies, old friends, and none of the pressures of competition.

In the end, Kerri decided to give gymnastics a bit more time to see if she could win another medal. Kerri spent three years bouncing between gyms, cities, and coaches, losing confidence along the way, partly because she didn't have Coach Bela to guide her. Kerri also had her share of bad luck, tearing a stomach muscle in a European meet, forcing her to endure six months of recuperation. Kerri decided to go home and spend time with her family.

That decision allowed her to finish high school with old friends. Kerri enjoyed her classes and got top grades, managing to squeeze in her gymnastic training before and after school.

Finally a normal teenager and living with her family again, and with a less brutal training schedule, Kerri seemed to thrive. Then came another setback— in a meet in 1994, Kerri was on the uneven bars when her grip slipped and she swung backward off the bar. She hit the mat painfully, hurting her back muscles, an injury that required another six months of recovery.

For most of her career, Kerri earned silver and bronze medals, often failing to win gold by just a fraction of a point, as if there were a mental barrier holding her back. She had been part of the 1992 Olympic team but it ended in frustration when she barely missed out on the chance to compete in the individual All-Around competition, losing to a competitor by .001 point. Now she was dealing with her second serious injury and she began to lose faith in her abilities.

"For so long, I put so much pressure on myself and it wasn't working," she says.

Kerri began meeting with sport psychologists, discussing her fears and goals. Over time, she started to see results from her therapy sessions.

"I became more confident," she says. "I finally learned that focusing on everyone else's performance—and what could go wrong for me—was not beneficial."

In 1995, Kerri graduated from her hometown high school in Tucson, Arizona. It likely helped that she was in a comfortable environment near supportive friends and family.

Enjoying her newfound focus and poise, Kerri won some competitions, including the America's Cup title in March 1996, returning her to the ranks of the elite members of the sport. Kerri put off starting college at UCLA to resume training with Coach Bela, who had ended his brief retirement. A shot at an Olympic medal seemed within reach. The big difference: She finally believed in herself.

"Everyone can tell you things, but until you believe it, it's not the same," she says. "I also knew it was my last year in competition, so I had everything to gain and nothing to lose . . . my goal was to make the Olympics but I realized life was going to go on either way. I had parents who loved me and I was going to college."

At the Olympic trials in Boston, Kerri earned a spot on the team with an impressive performance in all her rotations, taking the highest score in the vault and floor exercises.

As the Olympics approached, Kerri saw an individual medal as the one thing that could prove her ability and dedication once and for all. Skeptics worried she wasn't up to the challenge, but Kerri felt more confident than ever before, partly due to her conversations with her therapist.

As Dominique Moceanu, one of the team's golden girls, began the vault on July 23, 1996, Kerri wasn't even watching. It was the last apparatus left in the competition and the team's lead over Russia was so enormous their victory seemed assured.

"I was focused and in my zone, keeping my muscles loose and preparing," she says.

Then Kerri heard gasps from the crowd. Moceanu had fallen. Kerri stopped her preparations to watch Moceanu on the Georgia Dome's Jumbotron. Shockingly, she fell again.

"Dom was the darling of the Olympic games, she had never fallen on the vault," Kerri says, still amazed by the turn of events.

Most of the US's lead had evaporated. The gold medal would come down to Kerri's performance.

"The Americans could lose the gold medal," the television announcer said.

Referring to Kerri, he said: "She's the last to go, she's the only one who can do it."

In the stands, Kerri's parents looked tense as their daughter took a few last deep breaths.

"I didn't look at the scoreboard, but I thought, 'I can do this, I've done it all year, there's a reason I'm here,'" Kerri recalls. "I knew what to do."

She took off, launching a challenging routine that included a headspring and a twisting dismount as the crowd rose to its feet. As Kerri made her landing, however, she fell short, slipping and then falling on her backside. Kerri couldn't stick the landing.

She also heard a snap in her left ankle.

"Oh no!" the announcer exclaimed. "Three falls in a row for the Americans!"

It was Kerri's nightmare unfolding in the full glare of the world.

"I don't know the last time Kerri Strug did something like that," the announcer said. "This is her event."

"I was seriously embarrassed," Kerri says. "This was supposed to clinch it for us and I vaulted tens of thousands of times, and now I'm thinking, 'Here we go again.'"

Kerri didn't grimace or show signs of pain. But she began to limp as she walked off the mat. It was clear she was badly injured. Pain shot through Kerri's leg. She didn't realize it at the time, but she had suffered two torn ligaments in her ankle.

"This is scary," the television announcer said.

Kerri remembered how she had seriously hurt her

back just a few years earlier and began to think a gold medal wasn't meant to be.

"I'm the type of person who is 'Woe is me,' she says. "I thought 'Is this a sign from the man upstairs?'"

When Kerri's score, a weak 9.162, flashed on the Jumbotron it seemed the US gold medal was in serious jeopardy. Kerri still had her second vault ahead, but it wasn't clear she could go on. Kerri's parents covered their faces.

"It hurt and felt out of place, and it was scary not knowing what was wrong," she says.

Kerri's supporters rose to the occasion, trying to give her a boost. The US coaches encouraged her, as did her teammates.

"You can do it!" Coach Bela yelled out.

Kerri's head ached, her ankle throbbed, and it wasn't even clear if she could run. But Kerri made a decision. She'd push forward and do one more vault.

"I didn't want to go out like that," Kerri says. "I didn't want to be remembered for being injured."

She also didn't want the US team to be known as the squad that fell three times and blew a huge lead to lose the gold. Kerri's experience dealing with a grueling training regimen began to pay off, she says.

"All those injuries and competing in pain earlier in my career helped," she says. Coaches had "always pushed me past the point where I thought I could go, but it was a blessing in disguise."

Kerri had dreamed of winning an Olympic medal since she was five years old. She wasn't going to give up now.

"I was really hurt but I was just thinking about the gold medal," Kerri says. "I didn't think about quitting."

American team medics helped Kerri get to her feet as the crowd cheered wildly. The Russian team stopped to watch. Kerri began running down the runway on her damaged ankle for her second and final vault.

She realized she was in trouble right away.

"I felt pain and my ankle wasn't stable," Kerri says. "It felt like I was going to fall on my face [and] I felt slower. It just didn't feel right."

Somehow, Kerri remained on her feet and raced forward, picking up speed and launching herself high in the air. Relying on muscle memory and ignoring her pain, she pulled off a perfect back handspring onto the vault, descending toward the ground as many in the crowd held their breath. They knew how painful it would be when Kerri landed.

Improbably, Kerri landed on both feet without a stumble and raised her hands over her head to finish the vault with proper form. Just then, she heard another crack in her damaged left ankle. Instinctively, Kerri lifted her injured left leg, moving it behind her right as she hopped and shifted her weight to her healthy right leg. She even forced a smile on her face in the traditional post-performance pose.

Kerri held the pose long enough for the judges to give their marks. She then crumbled to the ground in agony as her coaches raced over to help her get off the mat.

A few minutes later, her score flashed for all to see.

"A 9.712, she has done it!" the announcer screamed. "Kerri Strug has won the gold medal for the American team!"

Kerri was carried off on a stretcher to seek medical

assistance as her teammates jumped for joy and the Russian gymnasts broke down in tears.

"The Georgia Dome is all at once in pandemonium and everyone is worried about Kerri Strug," the announcer said.

Before leaving for X-rays, Coach Bela scooped Kerri up, carrying her to the medal podium where she and the team received gold medals, as the crowd exploded in cheers.

Kerri's heroics brought fans to their feet and wowed television audiences around the world. Even as Kerri smiled for the cameras, inside she was dealing with mixed emotions, however.

She was thrilled to have won a gold medal, of course. That was her life's dream. But she was in a lot of pain. She also was dealing with deep disappointment. Kerri had expected to compete in individual events at the Olympics. Even after her fall, Kerri figured some rest, massage, and icing would enable her to go on. But it became clear that her injury was too severe for her to participate in more events. Her Olympic career likely was over.

"I shouldn't have fallen in the first place, this is what I spent my life preparing for," Kerri says. "I accomplished one goal, the team gold, but I was really upset I couldn't pursue my individual goals . . . I was really down."

Kerri worried she'd be known as the girl who fell in the Olympics. At the time, she didn't realize that she would instead be remembered as the brave young gymnast who refused to stay down.

Indeed, Kerri and her teammates were in the secluded Olympic Village and she didn't know the entire nation was cheering her, rather than focusing on her fall. A US Olympic official brought her a copy of the *USA Today* newspaper, pointing to the cover.

"You'll want to keep this," he said.

Kerri and her feat of courage were featured on the cover of the paper.

"It was a good feeling," she says.

Still, at the time, Kerri didn't fully grasp the significance of what she had done. Instead of taking pride in her amazing accomplishment, she continued to criticize herself even as she received acclaim from all over the world. Few had seen such a young person with so much mettle. Kerri became a national sports hero. She visited President Bill Clinton, appeared on television talk shows, and was on the cover of *Sports Illustrated* magazine, and, in the great tradition of star athletes, her face was plastered on the front of a Wheaties cereal box.

It took a while before Kerri could truly be proud of what she had accomplished.

"I was so focused on what was next and winning," she says. "I wish I had enjoyed the Olympics more than I did."

Eventually, after much self-reflection, Kerri learned some valuable lessons. She was so caught up in achieving her goals that she didn't understand that the journey to get to a certain destination can be even more valuable than the final result. Over time, she learned to treat herself with kindness. After all, very few people are ever in a position to compete in the Olympics. Falling or even failing in the Olympics should be a point of pride, not embarrassment, especially if the end result is winning a gold medal.

"Now I'm more thankful and appreciate that people mess up," she says.

Kerri also realized that had she and her teammates cruised to victory or if she had captured several individual gold medals, Kerri wouldn't have been able to inspire so many around the world with her resilience.

"Perseverance is a valuable characteristic," she acknowledges.

It's a trait Kerri finally appreciated about herself, and one she hopes others can learn from.

"I fell down but if this young girl can be tough and recover, so can others," she says.

Other life lessons also emerged from her experience.

"I gained an understanding that life doesn't always give you want you want. You think you know the path you want to take and how things will go." Yet, as Kerri discovered, it's rare that life doesn't take twists and turns that require grit and determination.

After the Olympics, Kerri graduated from Stanford University. Today, she lives in the Washington, D.C., area and gives motivational speeches around the country, sharing her experiences at the Olympics and more.

But she spends most of her time working and helping young people try to overcome their own challenges. In addition to being a mom to two young children, Kerri works as a program manager for the Office of Juvenile Justice and Delinquency Prevention, a division of the Department of Justice. She works with and advises programs for high-risk youth that receive federal funding, among other forms of aid.

"I spent most of my adolescence focused on me and my goals," she says. "I wanted to help others and serve in some capacity."

Just as with the Olympics, she says, she and others at the Department of Justice, "different people with different roles, work together to make America better."

When she speaks with young people, Kerri reminds them that success and accomplishment require practice, dedication, and perseverance.

"When you sacrifice so much and you finally do well, it feels really good," she says.

As Kerri learned after her moment of triumph, it's often our toughest setbacks that lead to our greatest victories.

AFTERWORD

As we spoke with the remarkable women featured in *Rising Above* it became clear that their athleticism and natural talent hadn't been enough to help them achieve greatness. Each star had overcome imposing obstacles at some point in their careers, a reminder that almost every life is filled with serious tests and challenges. In many ways, more than their abilities, it was those character-building moments that set them apart and allowed the women to develop into superstars.

Many of the athletes, including Serena and Venus Williams, confronted serious medical issues. Simone Biles, Ronda Rousey, and others faced humiliation due to their unique body types. Wilma Rudolph dealt with racism and Elena Delle Donne was impacted by the needs of a family member. Skeptics said Carli Lloyd and Kerri Strug, among others, wouldn't accomplish greatness. Bethany Hamilton and other athletes faced serious setbacks so sudden they had no time to prepare or adjust to their new circumstances. Yet, each of the women managed to rise above their difficult circumstances to excel in gymnastics, tennis, basketball, soccer, and more.

As we spoke with the stars and heard their life stories, some common themes emerged. The athletes often turned to others for help. Simone Biles worked with a psychologist, Carli Lloyd found a coach she trusted, while Swin Cash confided in an older mentor. The lesson: Turning to a friend, parent, therapist, or other person for help or guidance isn't a sign of weakness. Instead, it can be the best way to deal with life's trials.

The stars also shared an unwillingness to blame others for their difficulties. In fact, some said they began to become both better people and players when they stopped pointing the finger at others and accepted responsibility for their successes and failures.

"I had a revelation," Swin Cash told us. "I wouldn't

be a victim any longer . . . I had to look within myself and make things happen."

Simone Biles and others emphasized the importance of developing life goals and keeping them in focus, no matter how distracted one can get.

"Write them down," Simone told us. "And don't give up on them!"

Most of all, the stars emphasized the importance of believing in oneself and ignoring inevitable critics and skeptics.

"Always bet on yourself," Venus said to us. "Don't let outsiders bring negativity into your mind and your life."

Keep in mind what Kerri Strug, Wilma Rudolph, Bethany Hamilton and others discovered: Misfortune and sudden disappointments that appear to be blows can actually turn into big breaks.

It's our belief that everyone has a difference of some kind. Most of us will have to deal with huge disappointments at some point. But setbacks don't have to be roadblocks. Sometimes, they're even opportunities. We hope the stories from *Rising Above* can serve as useful life lessons for those facing their own challenges.

Gregory, Gabriel and Elijah Zuckerman

West Orange, NJ

May 2017

ACKNOWLEDGMENTS

We'd like to thank Venus Williams, Simone Biles, Carli Lloyd, Swin Cash, Kerri Strug, Bethany Hamilton and Mo'ne Davis all of whom generously took time to share thoughts, stories and lessons.

Brian Geffen is truly a remarkable editor. Supportive, enthusiastic and full of insight and wisdom. We thank you for the huge role you play in all our work. Our publisher, Michael Green, believed in this project from day one and we appreciate your continued support.

Susie, Hannah, Rebecca, Nathan (P.T.) and Liora cheer us from the sidelines and we love you guys. Josh Marcus provided necessary comic relief. Thanks as well to Monica for your hard work and being there for us.

Michelle, you're the true superstar of the family. Thank you for your love, wit, and kindness. Go, Yankees!

BIBLIOGRAPHY

Simone Biles

Simone Biles with Michelle Burford, *Courage to Soar: A Body in Motion, A Life in Balance*, Zondervan, 2016

Nick Zaccardi, "Simone Biles Recalls Being Called 'Too Fat' at Her Worst Meet," NBC Sports, November 16, 2016

Rose Minutaglio, "Simone Biles on Overcoming Body-Shaming from Coach," *People*, November 16, 2016

Pritha Sarkar, "Gymnastics: Bullies Are Tormenting Douglas, Says Mother," Reuters, August 14, 2016

Dvora Meyers, "Simone Biles' Mental Gymnastics," BuzzFeed, July 8, 2016

Linley Sanders, *Teen Vogue*, September 15, 2016

Alice Park, "The Olympic Gymnast Who Overcame a Drug-Addicted Mother," *Time*, June 3, 2016

Susan Rinkunas, "Gymnastics Star Simone Biles on Rio and Embracing Her Muscles," *New York*, July 13, 2016

Louise Radnofsky and Ben Cohen, "Simone Biles Wins Third Gold With Women's Vault Triumph," *Wall Street Journal*, August 14, 2016

Chelsea Hirsch, "Inside Gymnast Simone Biles' Tragic Early Days: Bio Mom Arrested for Stealing Baby Formula," Radar Online, August 11, 2016

Lonnae O'Neal, "The Difficulty of Being Simone Biles," *ESPN The Magazine*, July 6, 2016

Nicole Pelletiere, "Simone Biles Says 'Final Five' Will Take Vacation Together," ABC News, August 19, 2016, http://abcnews.go.com/Entertainment/simone-biles-return-rio/story?id=41509433

Elena Delle Donne

Sean Morrison, "Chicago Trades Elena Delle Donne for No. 2
Overall Pick, 2 Players," ABC Sports, https://abc7.com/sports
/chicago-trades-elena-delle-donne-for-no-2-overall-pick-2
-players/1733605/

Jere Longman, "At Pinnacle, Stepping Away from Basketball,"
New York Times, October 18, 2008

Graham Hays, "Finding Her Way Back Home," ESPN, December 7,
2012, http://espn.go.com/espn/eticket/story?page=elenaDonne

Taffy Brodesser-Akner, "The Audacity of Height," *ESPN The
Magazine*, November 22, 2016

Serena and Venus Williams

Serena Williams with Daniel Paisner, *My Life: Queen of the Court*,
Simon & Schuster, 2009

James Masters and Pat Cash, "Venus Williams: The
Champion Trying to Slam Sjögren's Syndrome, CNN, March
21, 2014, http://edition.cnn.com/2014/03/20/sport/tennis
/venus-williams-sjogrens-syndrome/

Dayna Evans, "Serena Williams Prefers to Be Known as One of the
Greatest Athletes of All Time," *New York*, July 7, 2016, http://
nymag.com/thecut/2016/07/serena-williams-best-female
-athlete.html

"Serena Williams Sits Down with Common to Talk about Race and
Identity," *The Undefeated*, December 19, 2016,
http://theundefeated.com/features/serena-williams-sits-down
-with-common-to-talk-about-race-and-identity/

Zoe Henry, "Venus Williams: Here's When It's OK to Fail," *Inc.*,
November 3, 2016

Jordan Crucchiola, "Serena Williams' Mom Gives Great Advice
on How to Handle Body Shamers," Good, July 11, 2016,

https://www.good.is/articles/serena-williams-wimbledon
-body-shaming

Mo'ne Davis

Kimberly Richards, "South Philly Girl, 10, Excels in Several
Sports," *Philadelphia Tribune*, December 14, 2011

Bethany Hamilton

Bethany Hamilton, *Soul Surfer*, MTV Books, 2004

Michael Lee, "The Great Escape," *Washington Post*, February 17,
2008

Victor Mather, "Bethany Hamilton, a Shark-Attack Survivor,
Reaches an Unlikely Crest," *New York Times*, May 31, 2016

Carli Lloyd

Carli Lloyd with Wayne Coffey, *When Nobody Was Watching*,
Houghton Mifflin Harcourt, 2016

Jose de Jesus Ortiz, "Lloyd's Quest for World Cup Title Forged by
2011 Setback," *Houston Chronicle*, June 6, 2015

Jeff Carlisle, "How Getting Cut Helped Carli Lloyd Refocus and
Find Her Spot on The USWNT," ESPN.com, June 3, 2015

Wilma Rudolph

Wilma Rudolph, *Wilma*, Signet, 1977

Kathleen Krull, *Wilma Unlimited*, Voyager, 2000

Ronda Rousey

Ramona Shelburne, "In Her Quest for Revenge and Pride, Ronda
Rousey Lost Her Own Way," ESPN, January 2, 2017

Gabrielle Olya, "Ronda Rousey Gets in Fighting Shape with
6-Hour Gym Sessions! Her Trainer Breaks Down Her Intense

Workout," *People*, July 26, 2016, http://www.people.com/
article/ronda-rousey-boxing-workout

Ronda Rousey, *My Fight/Your Fight*, Regan Arts 2015

Brian Martin, "Ronda Rousey: Pro Fight No. 3—Defeated Sarah
D'Alelio via Technical Submission (Armbar), 0:25, First
Round," *Los Angeles Daily News*, July 29 2015

Swin Cash

Swin Cash, *Humble Journey: More Precious Than Gold*, Empower-
ing You, 2013

Jeff Jacobs, "Mom's The Word," *Hartford Courant*, March 24, 2001

J. Brad McCollough, "At Olympics, Swin Cash has McKeesport on
Her Mind," Pittsburgh Post-Gazette, July 22, 2012

Nina Mandel, "WNBA veteran Swin Cash Draws Inspiration,
Toughness from Her Mom," *USA Today*, May 10, 2015

Seth Berman, "Swin Cash Leaving Her Mark on Liberty in Her
Last WNBA Season," *New York Times*, September 6, 2016

Kerri Strug

Rick Weinberg, "51: Kerri Strug Fights Off Pain, Helps US Win
Gold," ESPN, July 19, 2004, http://www.espn.com/espn
/espn25/story?page=moments/51

Kerri Strug: Official Web Site of Olympic Gold Medal Gymnast,
http://www.kerristrug.info/

INDEX